50 NEW BOBBIN LACE PATTERNS

50
NEW
BOBBIN
LACE
PATTERNS

Claire
Burkhard

B.T. Batsford Ltd · London

First published 1993
Reprinted 1994, 1995, 1996

Typeset by Servis Filmsetting Ltd, Manchester
and printed in Great Britain by
Butler & Tanner Ltd, Frome and London

Published by
B.T. Batsford Ltd
4 Fitzhardinge Street
London W1H 0AH

A catalogue record for this book is available from the
British Library

ISBN 0 7134 6985 4

CONTENTS

INTRODUCTION

When I started lacemaking, no lace books were on the market and the publications obtainable in libraries had patterns only for Torchon lace. In the intervening period, a large selection of books has been produced. Manuals and pattern collections with antique and modern designs for all kinds of bobbin laces are now available. Nevertheless many people making lace purely as a hobby still seem to be looking for patterns. Since I started designing patterns for the bulletin of the Federation of Swiss Lacemakers I have often been asked, 'Do you know a book with easy patterns?'

This book contains fifty patterns especially selected for lacemakers who like lace projects that require neither many years of experience, nor months of work. However, experts may also enjoy making a simpler piece of lace as a change from demanding projects. They will find suggestions here for large pieces as well as many useful ideas for small presents.

In order to test the degree of difficulty, some patterns were given to members of an evening class. The response was overwhelming – the lacemakers not only enjoyed experimenting but soon started making suggestions for further projects. Some patterns were designed to fit a certain table, window or dress. This collective enthusiasm often led to pieces much larger than the designer or the lacemaker would ever have dared to think of. The tutor of the lace class, my friend Ruth Jucker, has played a large part in achieving these good results and also in the mounting of the lace. To watch as several versions of a simple sketch are carried out and then to photograph all the attractive pieces is a most rewarding experience!

Due to the limited size of book pages some diagrams had to be scaled down. In those cases the percentage is indicated that will give a full-size reproduction corresponding to the quoted thread. Of course, lacemakers used to fine thread have the option of reducing the size of the diagrams to match their thread. In any case, the use of blue or green paper for copying patterns is recommended when white lace is planned.

Linen thread was mainly used (Swedish 'Bockens Knyppelgarn'), in sizes that are likely to be easily available. Please note that there is a difference of a third in thickness between 2-ply and 3-ply thread. Should only 2-ply thread be available when 3-ply thread (the traditional lace thread in Switzerland) is indicated, then a different count must be chosen: e.g. 60/3 can be replaced by 40/2. While the traditional indirect count for linen thread is based on the imperial system, the count for silk is based on the metric system. Thus a 70/3 silk is different to a 70/3 linen thread. The new direct count 'dtex' is used for fancy threads made of glittering synthetic fibres, but for traditional lace threads this system has still not been adopted.

In many cases the use of coloured thread is proposed, and the lacemaker should have no difficulty in visualizing the colours. The real problem with black and white photographs is the fact that the lovely shades of unbleached linen (popular in Switzerland) and the seductive shades of cream silk cannot be shown. Only a few of the patterns in this book are as white as the photographs may suggest.

Producing a lace book not only involves making a certain amount of lace, but also solving many technical problems concerning the text, diagrams and photography. I am much indebted to friends and family members for their assistance, and especially to the tutor of my local photography evening-class and to the members of the Zurich-Oerlikon lace group.

Abbreviations: R = Repeat
M = Middle
* = Sewing (marked only in special cases)

Diagram Interpretation

Half Stitch   **Whole Stitch**

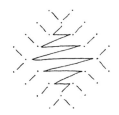   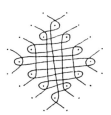

Linen threads: Bockens thread (made in Sweden) has been used throughout, except for 100/3, which is an Irish linen.

Other threads: When no make is specified, a thread was used that is not on the market any more. Suppliers of weaving threads may have a similar quality.

EINFÜHRUNG

Als ich mit Klöppeln anfing, gab es im Handel keine Bücher über Spitzen und in den Bibliotheken waren nur wenige Publikationen mit Torchon-Muster erhältlich. In der Zwischenzeit ist das Angebot gross und vielseitig – Anleitungen und Mustersammlungen für unzählige Arten von Klöppelspitzen, für historische und moderne Muster, stehen zur Verfügung. Trotzdem scheinen viele Klöpplerinnen immer auf der Suche nach Vorlagen zu sein. Seitdem ich für das Bulletin der Vereinigung der Schweizerischen Spitzenmacherinnen Muster zeichne, höre ich immer wieder die Frage: Können Sie mir ein Buch empfehlen mit einfachen Mustern?

Die fünfzig Klöppelbriefe dieses Buches sind speziell für Klöpplerinnen gedacht, die Muster schätzen, die weder langjährige Erfahrung, noch monatelange Arbeit verlangen. Aber auch erfahrene Klöpplerinnen, die schwierige Techniken beherrschen, machen gerne zur Abwechslung eine problemlose Spitze. Sie werden sowohl Vorschläge finden für grossformatige, wirkungsvolle Arbeiten, als auch viele verschiedene Ideen für kleine Geschenke.

Um den Schwierigkeitsgrad zu überprüfen, wurde ein Teil der Klöppelbriefe den Teilnehmerinnen eines Abendkurses vorgelegt. Das Echo war überwältigend – den Mitgliedern der Klöppelgruppe bereitet das Experimentieren offenbar viel Spass, zusätzlich wurden allerlei Anregungen und Wünsche übermittelt. So entstanden dann Muster, die für einen bestimmten Tisch, ein spezielles Fenster oder

Kleid bestimmt waren. Der Enthusiasmus der Gruppe führte zu Arbeiten in Formaten, an die sich weder die Zeichnerin noch die Ausführenden alleine heran gewagt hätten. Ohne Zweifel ist das gute Gelingen und die tadellose Montage der Spitzen der erfahrenen Kursleiterin, meiner Freundin Ruth Jucker, zu verdanken. Miterleben, wie aus einem bescheidenen Entwurf, verschiedene Varianten enstehen und dann all die schönen Sachen fotografieren – eine bereichende Erfahrung!

Das gegebene Format der Buchseiten lässt für einige Klöppelbriefe nur eine verkleinerte Wiedergabe zu. In solchen Fällen ist der Prozentsatz angegeben zur Wiederherstellung der Originalgrösse passend zum verwendeten Faden. Spitzenmacherinnen, die es vorziehen, mit feinem Faden zu arbeiten, haben selbstverständlich die Möglichkeit, die Vorlagen entsprechend zu verkleinern. Wenn weisse Spitzen geplant sind, ist es empfehlenswert, blaues oder grünes Papier für das Kopieren zu verwenden.

Es wurde hauptsächlich Leinenfaden verwendet, in Fadenstärken, die leicht zu beschaffen sein sollten ('Bockens Knyppelgarn' aus Schweden). Es ist zu beachten, dass der Unterschied zwischen 2-fach und 3-fach gezwirntem Material ungefähr einen Drittel in der Dicke ausmacht. Wenn an Stelle des vorgeschlagen 3-fach Faden (in der Schweiz traditionell) nur 2-fach gezwirnter Faden erhältlich ist, muss eine andere Nummer gewählt werden: Leinen 60/3 kann mit Leinen 40/2 ersetzt werden. Die überlieferte indirekte Numerierung für Leinen basiert auf dem (alte) englische Masssystem, die Numerierung für Seide auf dem metrische (Nm) System. Das heisst, dass Seide 70/3 nicht gleich ist wie Leinen 70/3. Die neue direkte Numerierung 'dtex' findet man bei Fantasiefaden aus glänzendem Kunstmaterial, aber leider ist dieses System für traditionelles Klöppelmaterial noch nicht eingeführt.

Verschiedentlich wird farbiger Faden vorgeschlagen und jederman wird sich die erwähnten Farben vorstellten können. Das eigentliche Problem der schwarzweiss Fotos ist die Tatsache, dass die schönen Naturfarben, ungebleichtes Leinen (in der Schweiz sehr beliebt) und die verführerischen Cremetöne der Seide nicht gezeigt werden können. Nur wenige Spitzen sind so weiss, wie sie auf den Bildern erscheinen.

Für die Herstellung eines Klöppelbuches braucht es nicht nur eine Menge Spitzen, sondern es müssen noch allerlei Knacknüsse technischer Art gelöst werden, sei es beim Texterfassen, beim Zeichnen oder Fotografieren. Ich möchte allen beteiligten Freunden und Familienmitgliedern für ihre Unterstützung danken, ganz besonders auch dem Leiter des Abendkurses für Fotografie und der Klöppelgruppe von Zürich-Oerlikon.

Erläuterungen zu den Klöppelbriefen

Halbschlag

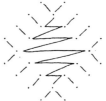

Leinenschlag

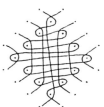

Leinenfaden: Es wurde immer die Marke 'Bockens' aus Schweden verwendet, nur der Zwirn 100/3 stammt aus Irland.

Andere Fäden: Wenn keine Marke angegeben ist, handelt es sich um Material, das nicht mehr im Handel ist. Die Lieferanten von Webgarn führen ähnliches Material.

Abkürzungen: R = Rapport
M = Mitte
* = anhäkeln (nur in speziellen Fällen markiert)

10

INTRODUCTION

Lorsque j'ai commencé à faire de la dentelle aux fuseaux, il n'y avait pas de livres de dentelle sur le marché, et les publications trouvées dans les bibliothèques ne contenaient que des modèles du genre Torchon. Entretemps un grand choix de livres a été édité – des manuels et des collections de modèles de tous les genres pour dentelles anciennes et modernes. Néanmoins beaucoup de dentellières faisant de la dentelle pour leur plaisir semblent être continuellement à la recherche de modèles. Depuis que je dessine des modèles pour le bulletin de la Fédération des Dentellières Suisses on me demande souvent: connaissez-vous un livre avec des modèles faciles?

Ce livre contient cinquante modèles destinés spécialement aux dentellières qui apprécient des ouvrages ne demandant ni des années d'expérience ni des mois de travail. Mais aussi les dentellières expérimentées aiment faire un ouvrage simple de temps à autre. Elles trouveront des propositions pour des pièces large d'un bel effet, ainsi qu'un choix intéressant d'idée pour la confection de petits cadeaux.

Afin de contrôler le degré de difficulté, une partie des modèles a été donnée aux membres d'un cours de dentelle. L'écho a été impressionnant – non seulent les dentellières se sont laissé prendre au jeu de la découverte, mais elles ont saisi l'occasion de faire des propositions pour des projets supplémentaires. C'est ainsi que des modèles correspondant à la grandeur d'une certaine table, d'une fenêtre ou d'une robe ont été conçus. L'enthusiasme collectif est a l'origine de plusieurs grandes pièces que ni la dessinatrice, ni les dentellières n'auraient oser prévoir. Sans doute, la monitrice, mon amie Ruth Jucker, a contribué largement au bons résultats et au montage impeccable. Assister au développement de plusieurs variantes à partir d'un simple croquis et en suite photographier toutes les belles choses – quelle expérience enrichissante!

Le format donné des pages du livre a pour conséquence que quelques dessins ont dû être réduits. Dans ces cas le pourcentage nécessaire est indiqué qui reproduira le format d'origine correspondant au fil utilisé. Les dentellières habituées à du fil fin ont la possibilité de choisir un format réduit correspondant à leur matériel. De toute manière l'utilisation de papier bleu ou vert pour copier les modèles est recommandable quand une dentelle blanche est projetée.

C'est surtout du fil de lin qui a été utilisé, en grosseur qui devraient être facile à obtenir ('Bockens Knyppelgarn' de Suède). Il faut tenir compte du fait qu'il y a une différence de grosseur d'un tiers entre le retors à deux brins et le retors à trois brins. Au cas ou le retors à trois brins (le fil à dentelle traditionel en Suisse) n'est pas en stock, il faut choisir un autre numéro: le lin 60/3 peut être remplacé par le lin 40/2. Le numérotage indirecte du lin se base sur le système anglais (ancien), le numérotage indirecte de la soie se base sur le système métrique. Ainsi un fil de soie 70/3 n'est pas indentique à un fil de lin 70/3. Le nouveau numérotage directe 'dtex' est utilisé pour les fils de phantaisie en matériel brillant synthétique, mais pour les fils à dentelle traditionels ce système n'a pas encore été adopté.

A différentes reprises du fil de couleur est proposé et, nul doute, il est possible de se représenter les couleurs mentionnées. Le vrai problème des photos en noir en blanc est le fait qu'il n'est pas possible reproduire la couleur naturelle du lin non-blanchi (très en vogue en Suisse) ni les tons crèmes séduisants de la soie. Peu de dentelles sont aussi blanches que les photos semblent suggérer.

Préparer un livre de dentelle ne représente pas seulement la confection d'un certain nombre de dentelles, mais aussi le dénouement de maintes autres problèmes concernant le texte, le dessin et la photographie. Je tient à remercier amis et membres de famille de leur soutient, tout spécialement le moniteur du cours de photographie et les dentellières du groupe de Zurich-Oerlikon.

Explications concernant les modèles

Demi point   **Mat**

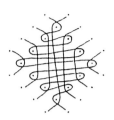

Fils de lin: Il s'agit toujours de la marque 'Bockens' de Suède, seulement le retors 100/3 provient d'Irlande.

Autres fils: Quand la marque n'est pas indiquée, il s'agit de fils qui n'est plus sur le marché. Les fournisseurs de fils à tisser sont la source de fils analogues.

Abbréviations: R = rapport
M = milieu
* = point de raccroc (sont seulement marqués les cas spéciaux)

LACE TO WEAR

SPITZEN ZUR KLEIDUNG
DENTELLES D'HABILLEMENT

1 Small Rhombus

The rows of rhombuses can be arranged in several ways, depending on the projected width. The Torchon ground may be replaced by a fancy stitch.

1a Scarf: 2 × 11 pairs, 'Pagoda' silk (or fine wool), pricking 125%

1b Bookmark: 12 pairs, linen 60/3, pricking 100%

---

1 Kleiner Rhombus

Die Reihen mit den Rhomben können auf verschiedene Arten angeordnet werden, je nach vorgesehener Breite. Der Torchon Grund kann mit einem Fantasiemuster ersetzt werden.

1a Halstuch: 2 × 11 Paare 'Pagoda' Seide (oder feine Wolle), Klöppelbrief 125%

1b Buchzeichen: 12 Paare, Leinen 60/3, Klöppelbrief 100%

---

1 Le Petit Losange

Les rangées de losanges peuvent être disposées de différentes manières, selon la largeur prévue. Le fond Torchon peut être remplacé par un point de fantaisie.

1a Echarpe: 2 × 11 paires, soie 'Pagoda' (ou laine fine), piquée 125%

1b Signet: 12 paires, lin 60/3, piquée 100%

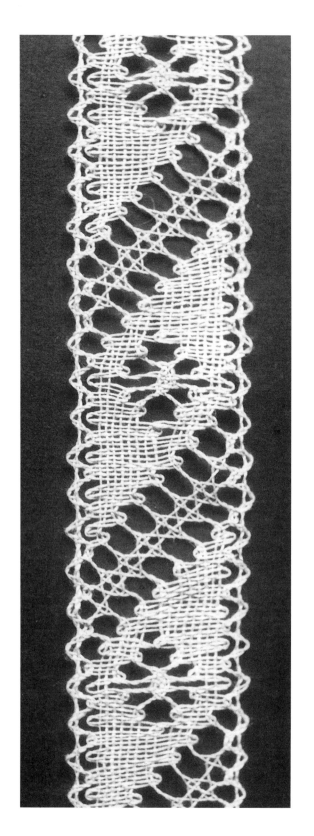

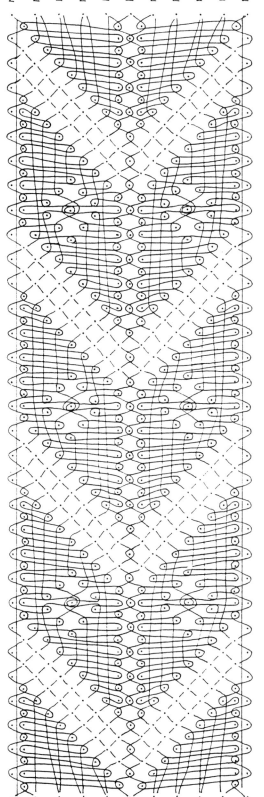

2 2 2 2 2 2 2 2 2 2 2

1a

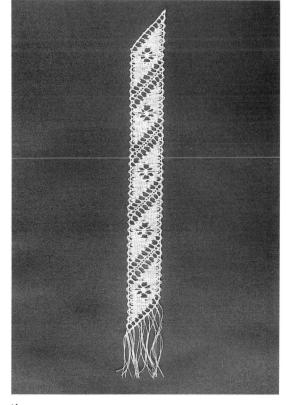

1b

2 Diagonal Pattern

There are two versions of this geometric pattern. The tie is made of two separate pieces, joined by overlapping in the middle (at the back). The one-sided collar starts at the waist and ends at the seam on the shoulder.

2a Tie: 18–20 pairs, silk No. 100/3 (optional gimp)
2b Collar: 16 + 10 pairs, linen 35/2

---

2 Diagonalmuster

Es gibt zwei Versionen zu diesem geometrischen Muster. Für die Kravatte wurden zwei Teilen in der Mitte (hinten) übereinander genäht. Der einseitige Kragen wird von unten nach oben gearbeitet und endet an der Schulternaht.

2a Kravatte: 18–20 Paare, Seide Nm 100/3 (Konturfaden fakultativ)
2b Kragen: 16 + 10 Paare, Leinen 35/2

---

2 Modèle diagonal

Ce modèle géométrique existe en deux versions. Pour la cravate, les deux pièces confectionnées séparément sont cousues l'une sur l'autre au milieu (du dos). Le demi-col est commencé à la taille et il finit à la couture sur l'épaule.

2a Cravate: 18–20 paires, soie Nm 100/3 (fil de contour facultatif)
2b Col: 16 + 10 paires, lin 35/2

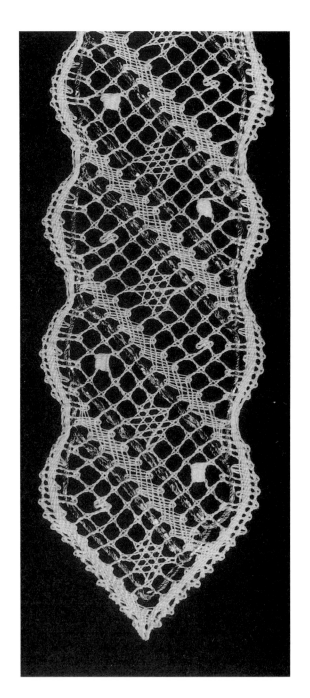

2a

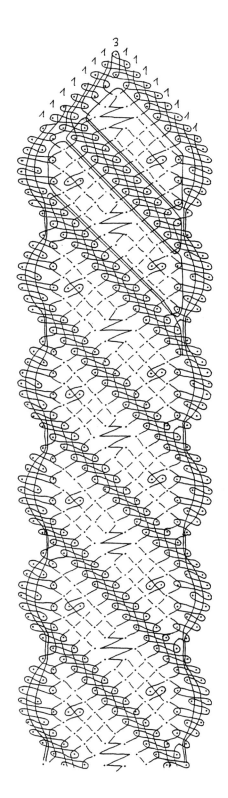

2a The tie, worked by Getrud Keel, is made of black silk with two additional edge pairs and a blue gimp that matches the colour of the blouse.

2a Die Kravatte, von Getrud Keel, aus schwarzer Seide geklöppelt, hat zwei zusätzliche Randpaare und einen blauen Konturfaden, der zur Farbe der Bluse passt.

2a La cravate en soie noire, exécutée par Getrud Keel, a deux paires supplémentaires dans le bord et un fil de contour bleu, assorti à la couleur de la blouse.

2b The wine-red dress with the collar in creamy linen is the work of Margrit Ebner.

2b Das weinrote Kleid mit dem Kragen aus Leinen in creme ist das Werk von Margrit Ebner.

2b La robe rouge-bordeaux garni d'un col en lin couleur crème et l'oeuvre de Margrit Ebner.

2b

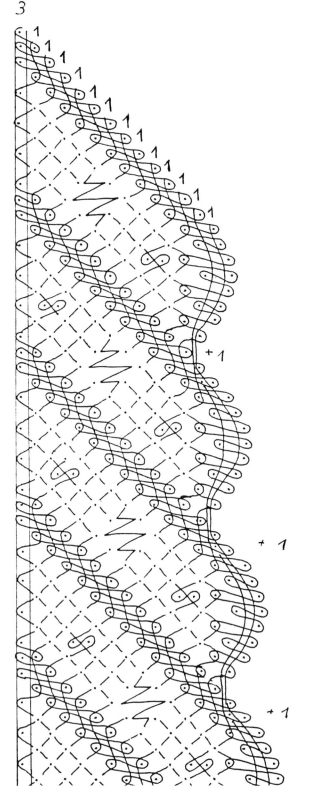

2b

+ 1

+ 1

+ 1

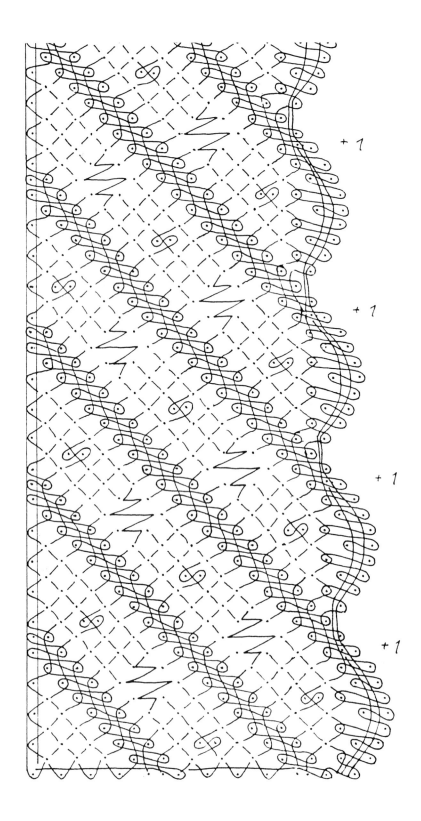

+ 1

+ 1

+ 1

+ 1

3 Daisy

For a collar 26 to 28 repeats will be necessary. A complete circle for a round mat consists of 36 repeats. The straight version can be used in many ways – a small ruffled collar can be adapted to different sizes.

3a Collar: 19 pairs, linen 40/3 or 35/2
3b Ruffled collar and 3-D flower:
    14 pairs

3 Gänseblümchen

Für einen Kragen muss man mit 26 bis 28 Rapporten rechnen. Der komplette Ring für ein rundes Deckchen besteht aus 36 Rapporten. Die gerade Version kann auf verschiedene Arten angewendet werden – eine kleine Krause als Kragen passt zu verschiedenen Grössen.

3a Kragen: 19 Paare, Leinen 40/3 oder 35/2
3b Krause und dreidimensionale Blume:
    14 Paare

3 La Paquerette

Pour un col il faut compter 26 à 28 rapports. Le cercle complet consiste de 36 rapports. La version droite peut être utilisée de plusieurs manières – une collerette s'adapte à différentes grandeurs.

3a Col: 19 paires, lin 40/3 ou 35/2
3b Collerette et fleur à trois dimensions:
    14 paires

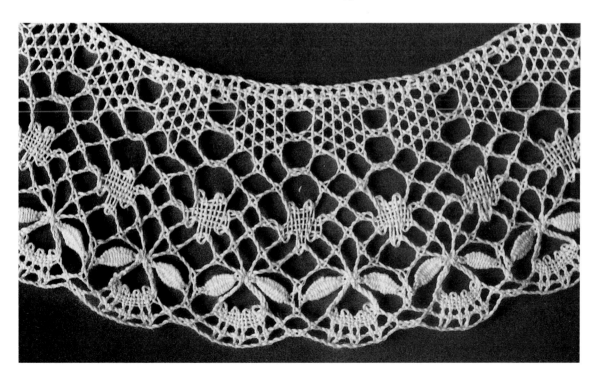

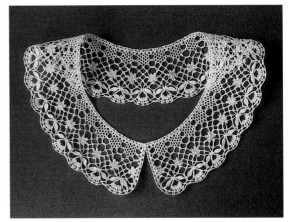

3a

3a

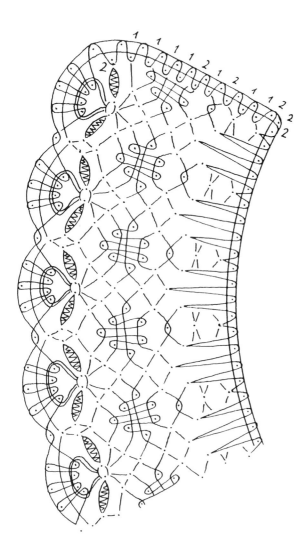

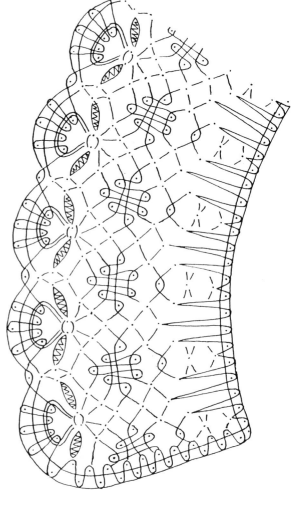

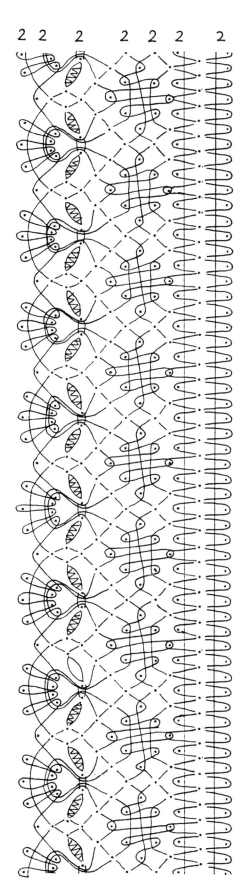

3b The ruff and sweater were worked by Silvia Huber.

3b Die Krause und der Pullover sind von Silvia Huber gearbeitet.

3b La collerette et le pullover sont exécutés par Silvia Huber.

3b

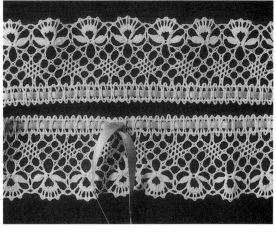

3b

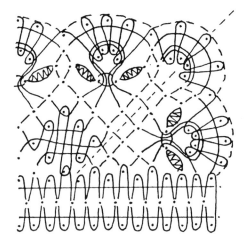

3b

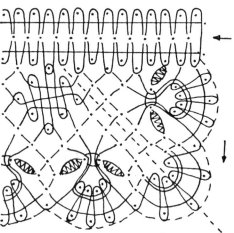

3c Corner for a mat
   Ecke für eine Decke
   L'angle pour un napperon

Alternative ending
Anderes Endstück
Autre manière de finir

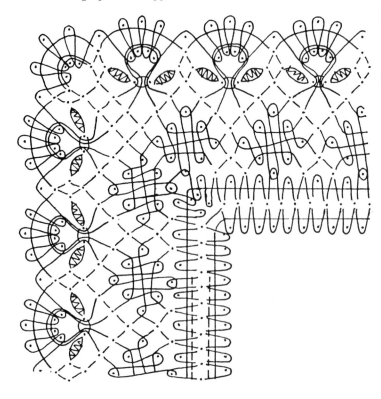

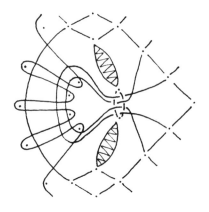

4 Snail

This narrow lace can easily be bent, providing the edge pair is treated as a gimp (fig. B). By pulling the 'gimp' pair gently, the lace can be made into the required shape.

7 pairs, linen 60/2

4 Schnecke

Diese schmale Spitze lässt sich leicht biegen, wenn das Randpaar wie ein Konturfaden (Fig. B) geführt wird. Man kann am 'Konturfadenpaar' ziehen bis die gewünschte Form erreicht ist.

7 Paare, Leinen 60/2

4 L'Escargot

Cette dentelle étroite s'adapte aisément à une courbe, à condition de traité la paire du bord comme un bourdon (fil de contour, fig. B). La forme désirée s'obtient en tirant sur la paire traitée en 'fil de contour'.

7 paires, lin 60/2

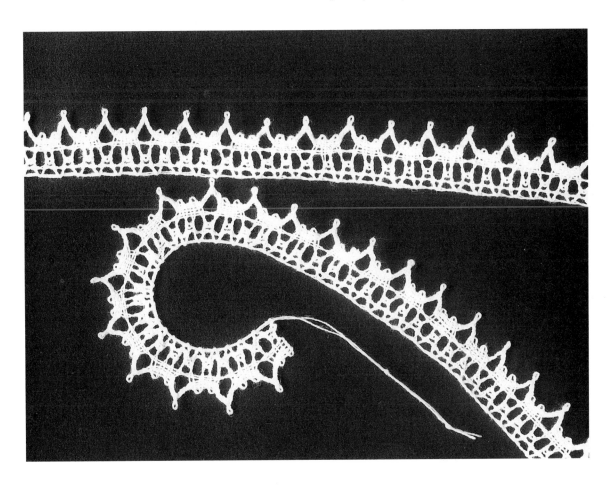

fig. A

fig. B

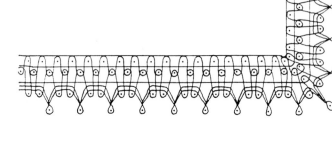

5 V-Pattern

Acute angles are uncommon in Torchon lace. This pattern demonstrates that such angles can be worked by using the 'sewing' method instead of using additional pairs.

19–20 pairs, linen 35/2 or 40/3

5 V-Muster

Spitze Winkel sind bei Torchon Spitzen eher ungewöhnlich. Dieses Muster zeigt, dass solche Winkel mit Hilfe der 'Häkeltechnik' ausgeführt werden können, statt zusätzliche Paare zu benützen.

19–20 Paare, Leinen 35/2 oder 40/3

5 Modèle en V

Les dentelles Torchon à angles aigus sont inhabituelles. Ce modèle prouve qu'il est possible d'exécuter cet angle en utilisant quelques points de raccroc, au lieu d'utiliser des paires supplémentaires.

19–20 paires, lin 35/2 ou 40/3

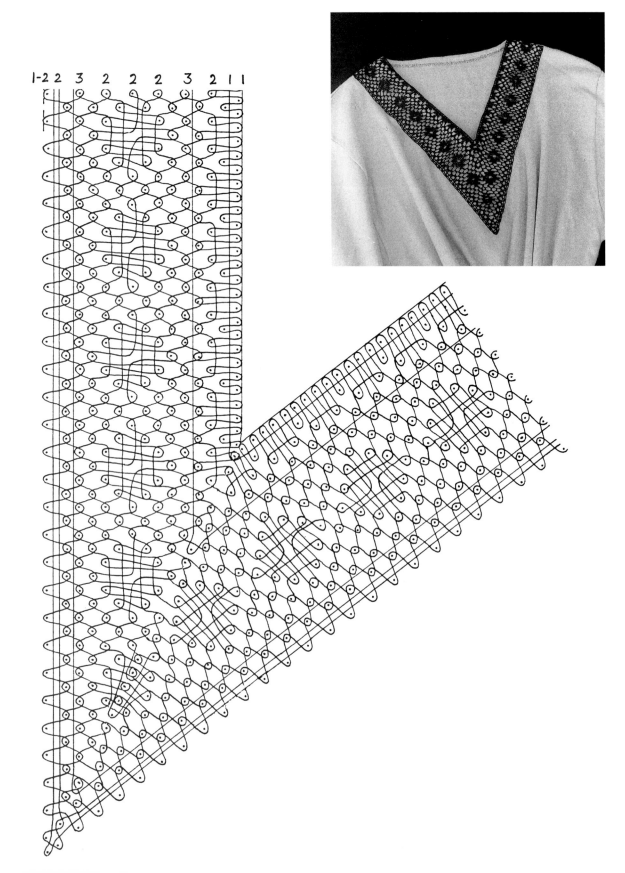

B

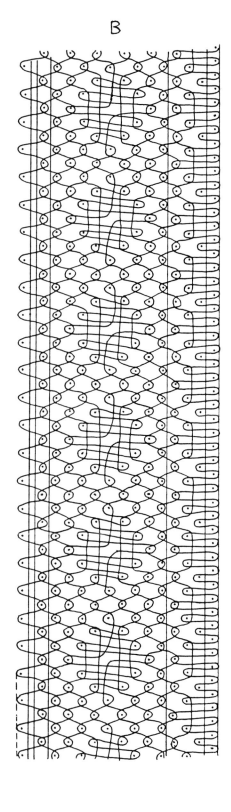

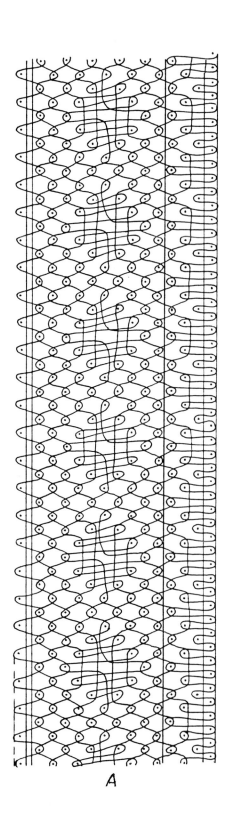

A

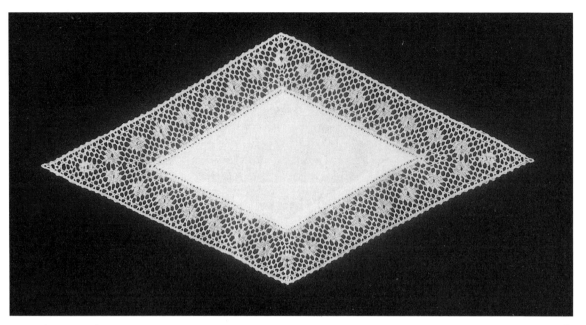

5a The lace for the table-mat was worked and mounted by Hanna Ziegler.

5a Die Spitze für die Decke ist von Hanna Ziegler geklöppelt und montiert.

5a La dentelle du napperon est exécutée et montée par Hanna Ziegler.

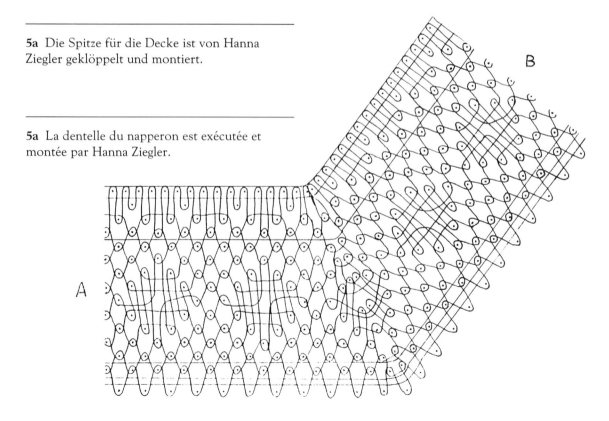

6 Giant Flower

Advanced lacemakers may use finer thread and add other fillings. Nevertheless it is possible to make an attractive piece by using only basic stitches.

Tape: 4–5 pairs, linen 60/3
Ground worked in sections of 10 pairs (see close-up of the wrong side of the lace)

6 Riesenblume

Fortgeschrittene Klöpplerinnen werden feineren Faden wählen und verschiedene Ziergründe anwenden. Trotzdem ist es möglich, mit einfachen Mitteln ein ansprechendes Stück herzustellen.

Band: 4–5 Paare, Leinen 60/3
Grund in Streifen mit 10 Paaren gearbeitet (siehe Nahaufnahme der Rückseite der Spitze)

6 La Fleur géante

Les expertes utiliseront du fil plus fin et ajouteront des fonds différents. Néanmoins il est possible de faire une pièce décorative avec des moyens simples.

Lacet: 4–5 paires, lin 60/3
Fond exécuté en sections de 10 paires (voir gros plan de l'envers de la dentelle)

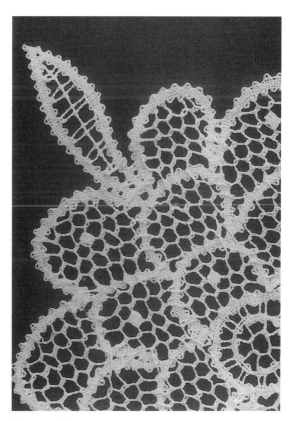

Wrong side
Rückseite
L'envers de la dentelle

7 Peacock Feather

The tie is made longer by adding some repeats of the narrow section. The main motif of the handkerchief corner corresponds to four repeats of the small edging.

7a Tie: 12 pairs, silk No. 70/3 (linen 60/3, pricking 111%)
7b Handkerchief: 14 pairs, silk No. 70/3
7c Square motif: 12 pairs, linen 60/3

---

7 Pfauenfeder

Die Kravatte wird verlängert, indem einige Rapporte des schmalen Teiles wiederholt werden. Das Hauptmotiv der Taschentuchecke entspricht vier Rapporten des Spitzchens.

7a Kravatte: 12 Paare, Seide Nm 70/3 (Leinen 60/3, Vorlage 111%)
7b Einstecktuch: 14 Paare, Seide Nm 70/3
7c Viereckiges Motiv: 12 Paare, Leinen 60/3

---

7 La Plume de paon

La cravate est ralongée en répétant quelques rapports de la partie étroite. Le motif principal de l'angle du mouchoir correspond à quatre rapports de la petite bordure.

7a Cravate: 12 paires, soie Nm 70/3 (lin 60/3, piquée 111%)
7b Pochette: 14 paires, soie Nm 70/3
7c Motif carré: 12 paires, lin 60/3

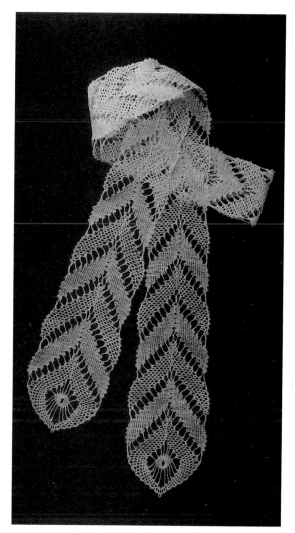

7a

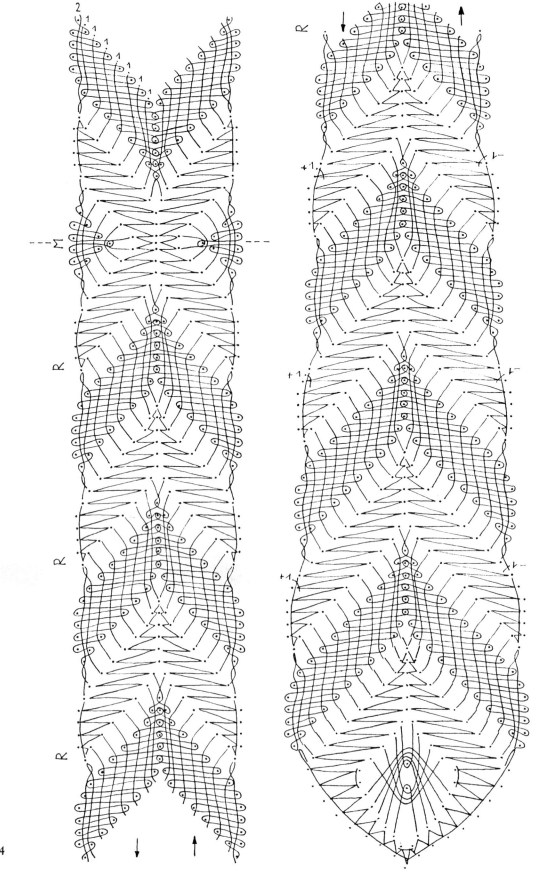

34

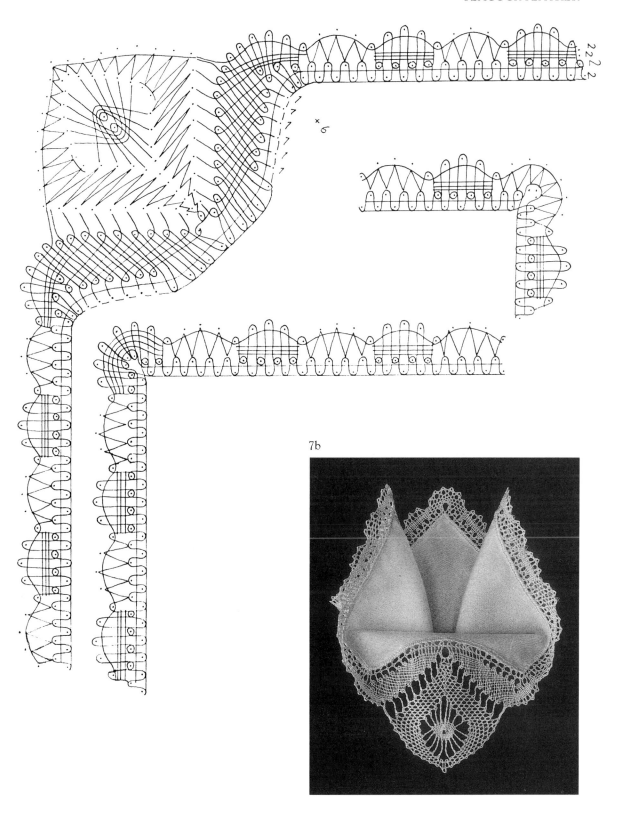

7b

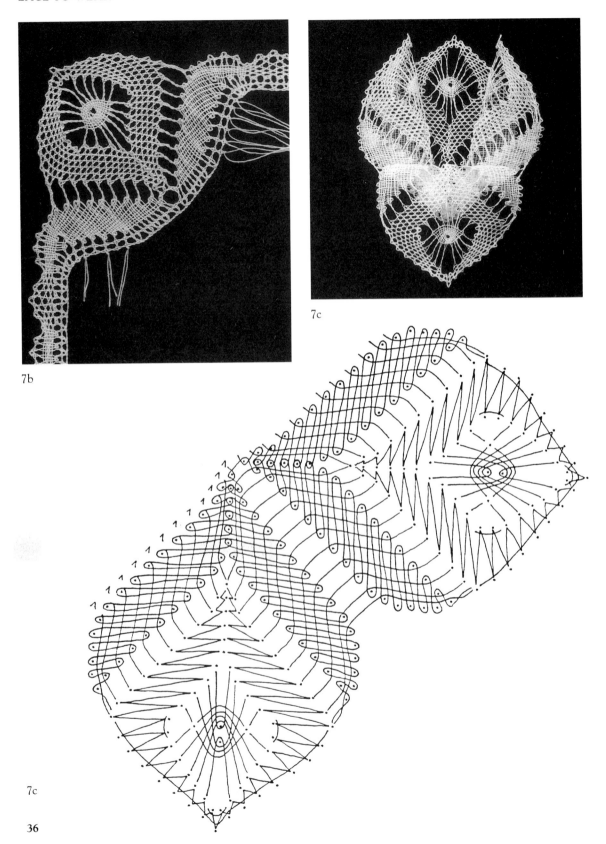

7b

7c

7c

8 Ladybird

Insertion and edging – the classic pair
for many purposes.

20 pairs/17 pairs, linen 60/2
2 gimps (40/3 double)

---

8 Marienkäfer

Entredeux und Kante – das klassische Paar für
viele Anwendungen.

20 Paare/17 Paare, Leinen 60/2
2 Konturfäden (40/3 doppelt)

---

8 La Coccinelle

Entredeux et bordure – la paire classique pour
maintes emplois.

20 paires/17 paires, lin 60/2
2 fils de contour (40/3 double)

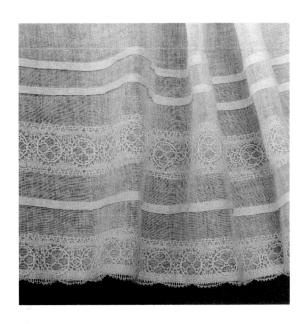

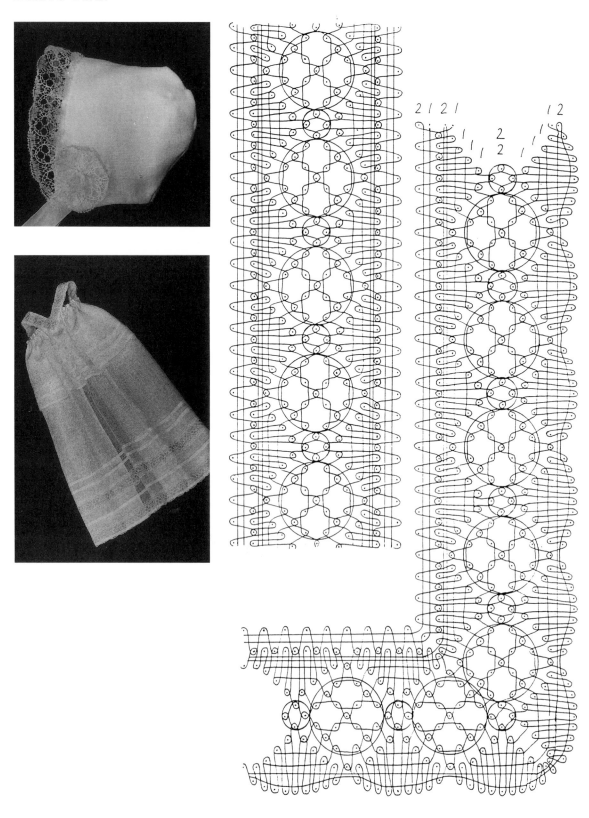

9 Thistle

For the large collar 20 repeats of the pattern are necessary. For a fan 12 repeats (including the two halves of the motif at the beginning and the end) correspond to a semi-circle.

9a Collar: 14 pairs, silk No. 200/6, pricking 100%
9b Fan: 14 pairs, silk No. 70/3, pricking 88%

9 Distel

Für den grossen Kragen werden 20 Rapporte benötigt. Für einen Fächer ergeben 12 Rapporte (die zwei halben Motive am Anfang und am Ende mitgezählt) einen Halbkreis.

9a Kragen: 14 Paare, Seide Nm 200/6, Klöppelbrief 100%
9b Fächer: 14 Paare, Seide Nm 70/3, Klöppelbrief 88%

9 Le Chardon

Pour le grand col il faut compter 20 rapports. Pour l'éventail 12 rapports (y compris les deux demi motifs du commencement et de la fin) forment un demi-cercle.

9a Col: 14 paires, soie Nm 200/6, piquée 100%
9b Eventail: 14 paires, soie Nm 70/3, piquée 88%

9a

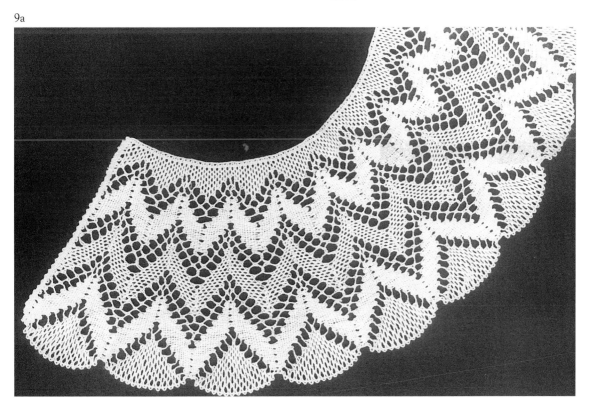

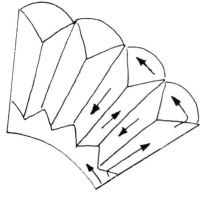

9a

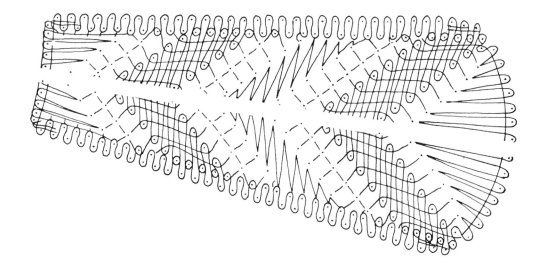

9b The lilac silk fan was made by Ruth Jucker.

9b Ruth Jucker hat den lila Seidenfächer hergestellt.

9b C'est Ruth Jucker qui a fait l'éventail en soie lila.

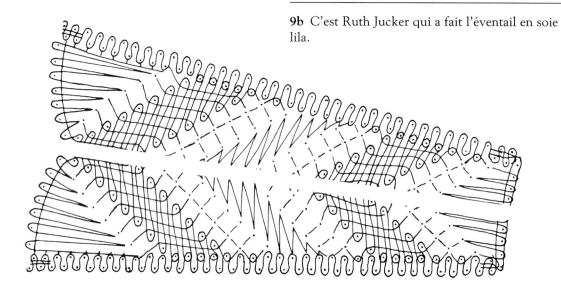

9b

10 Magic Tape

Few bobbins for a large surface – a tape with 'leaves' incorporated by an unusual method. The size of the pattern had to be reduced from A3 to A4.

10a Cuff: 6 pairs, linen 60/3, pricking 141%

10c Large collar: 2 × 6 pairs, linen 60/3, pricking 141%

10 Zauberband

Wenige Klöppel für eine grosse Fläche – ein Band mit 'Blättchen', eingearbeitet nach einer ungewöhnlichen Methode. Das Format des Musters musste von A3 auf A4 reduziert werden.

10a Manschette: 6 Paare, Leinen 60/3, Klöppelbrief 141%

10c Grosser Kragen: 2 × 6 Paare, Leinen 60/3, Klöppelbrief 141%

10 Le Lacet magique

Peu de fuseaux pour une grande surface – un lacet orné de petits 'feuilles' incorporées d'une manière inédite. Le format du modèle a dû être réduite de A3 à A4.

10a Manchette: 6 paires, lin 60/3, piquée 141%

10c Grand col: 2 × 6 paires, lin 60/3, piquée 141%

10a

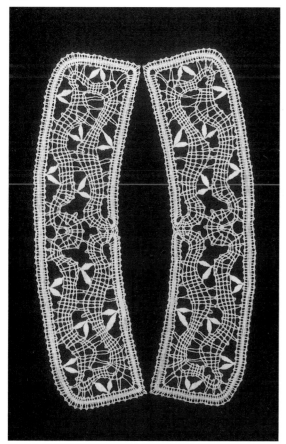

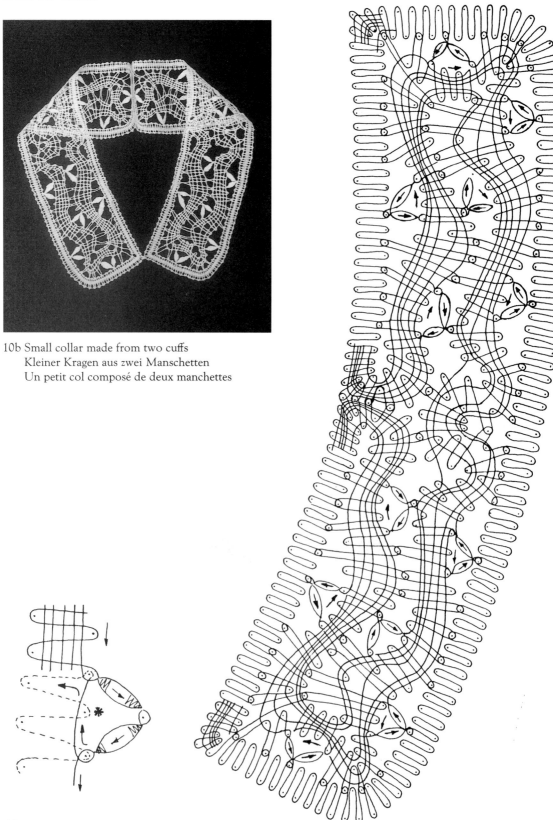

10b Small collar made from two cuffs
   Kleiner Kragen aus zwei Manschetten
   Un petit col composé de deux manchettes

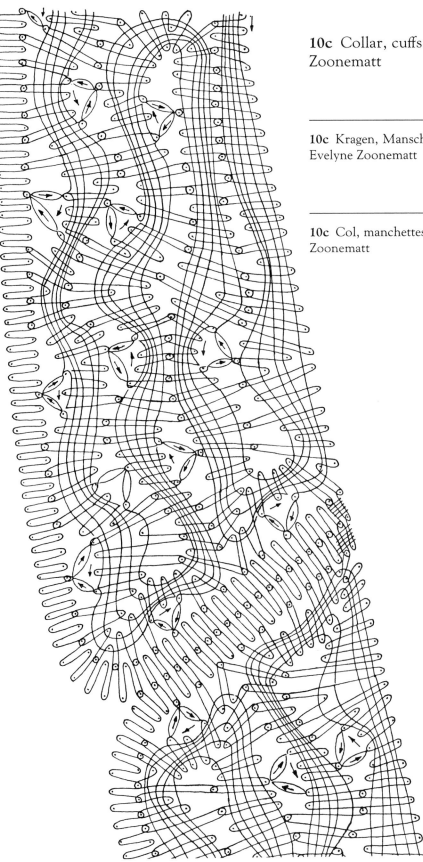

10c Collar, cuffs and jacket by Evelyne Zoonematt

10c Kragen, Manschetten und Jacke von Evelyne Zoonematt

10c Col, manchettes et jaquette d'Evelyne Zoonematt

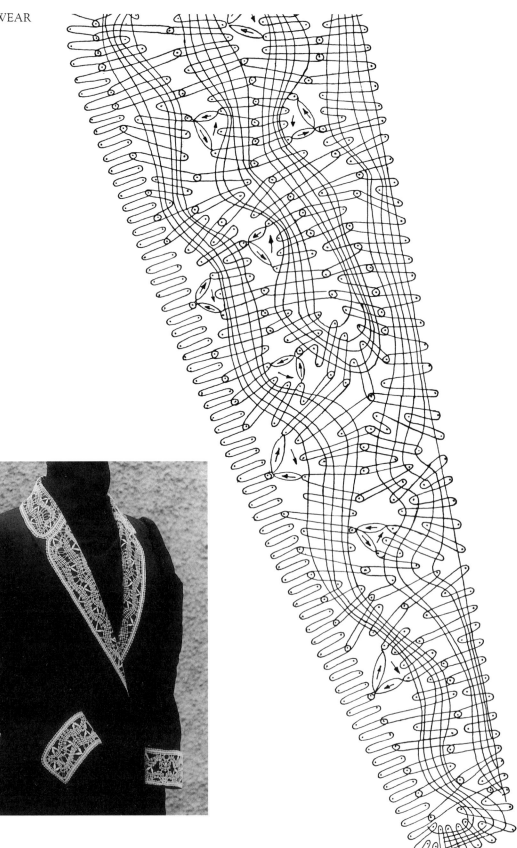

10c

11 Twig

This simple pattern of alternating clothstitch leaves has an edge which may be dropped when butterflies (pattern 12) or birds (pattern 18) are added, as in photograph 11a on p. 48.

22 pairs, linen 40/3

11 Zweig

Der Rand dieses einfachen Musters aus Leinenschlag-Blättern kann weggelassen werden, wenn Schmetterlinge (Muster 12) oder Vögel (Muster 18) dazukommen (siehe Fotografie 11a auf Seite 48).

22 Paare, Leinen 40/3

11 Le Rameau

Le bord de ce modèle simple à feuilles en mat peut être omis quand des papillons (modèle 12) ou des oiseaux (modèle 18) sont ajoutés (voir photographie 11a à la page 48).

22 paires, lin 40/3

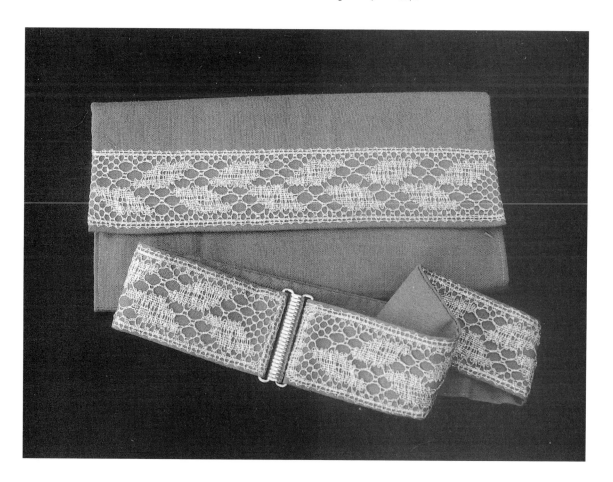

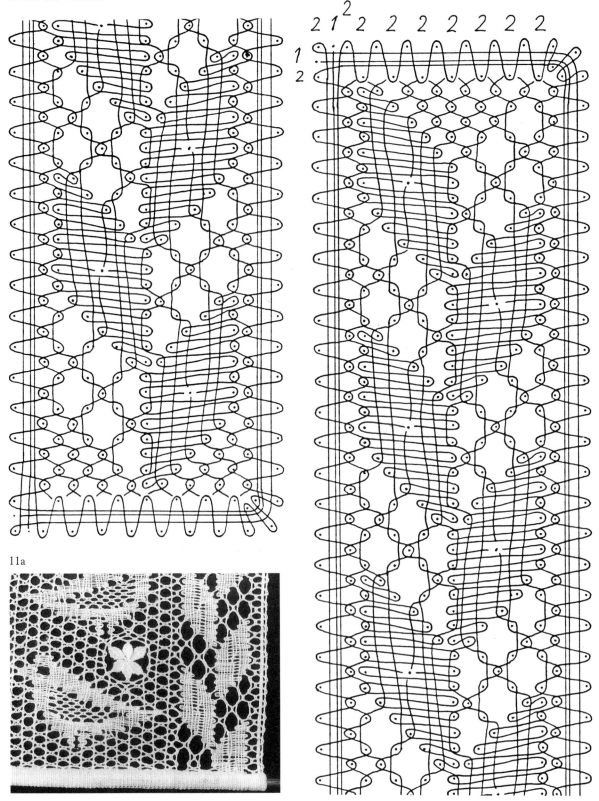

11a

Lace for a Window

Window

SPITZEN FÜR EIN FENSTER
DENTELLE POUR UNE FENÊTRE

12 Butterflies

The edge of the lace can be dropped or replaced by pattern No. 11. In the clothstitch area various stitches may be added to make a plain pattern more attractive; for butterflies in different colours only one pair of bobbins is non-continuous (see page 54).

48 (or 2 × 24) pairs, linen 40/3 or 35/2

---

12 Schmetterlinge

Der Rand dieser Spitze kann weggelassen oder durch Muster Nr. 11 ersetzt werden. Im Leinenschlag können Verzierungen eingearbeitet werden, damit eine einfarbige Spitze interessanter wird; bei Schmetterlingen in verschiedenen Farben ist nur ein Klöppelpaar nicht durchgehend (siehe Seite 54).

48 (oder 2 × 24) Paare, Leinen 40/3 oder 35/2

---

12 Les Papillons

La bordure de cette dentelle peut être omise ou remplacée par le modèle no. 11. La surface en mat peut être variée de manière à rendre une dentelle unie plus intéressante; uniquement une paire de fuseaux doit être interrompue pour les papillons de couleurs différentes (voir la page 54).

48 (ou 2 × 24) paires, lin 40/3 ou 35/2

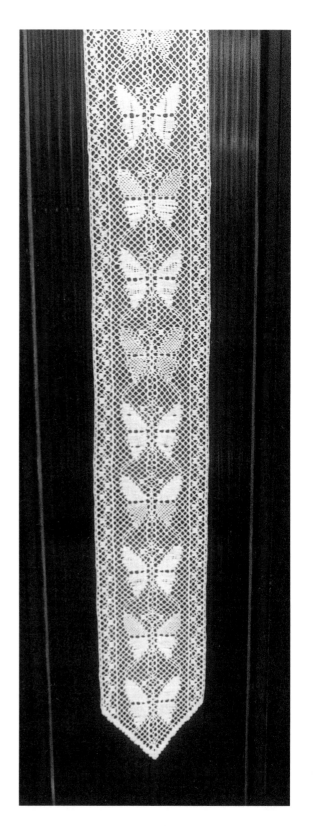

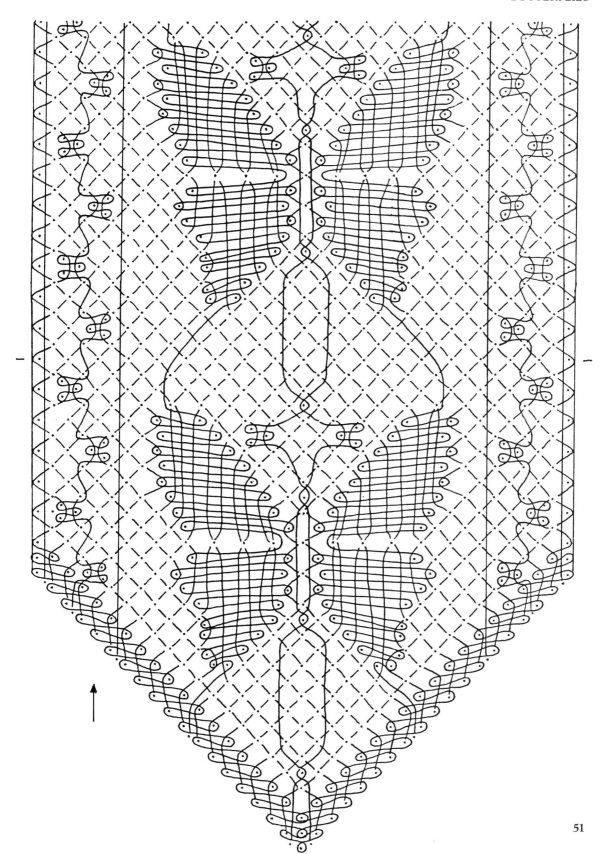

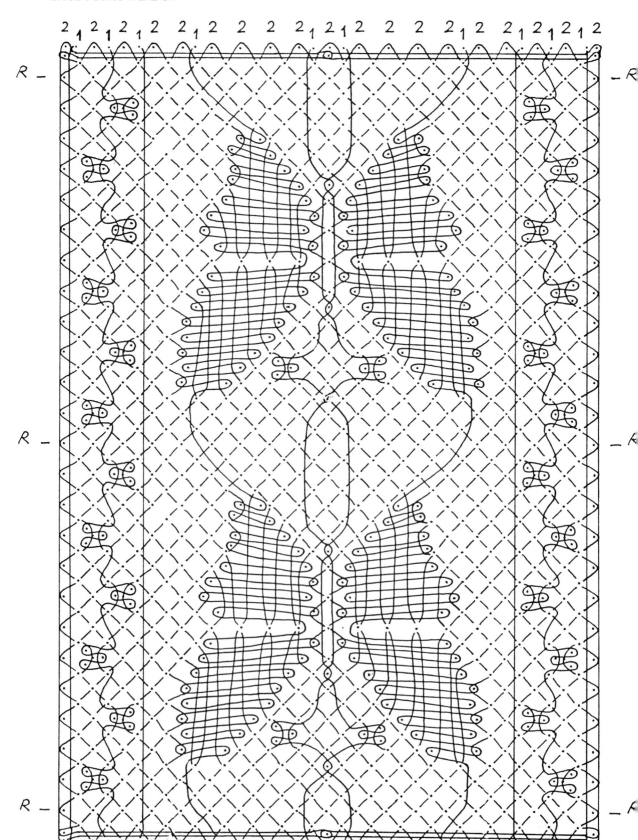

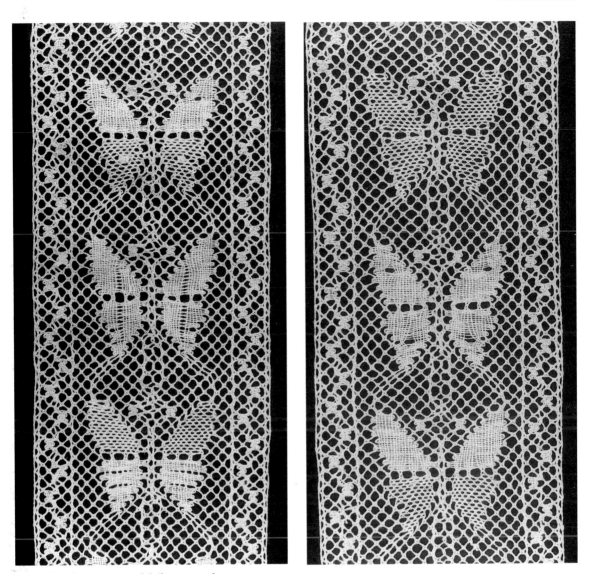

Butterflies showing use of different stitches
Schmetterlinge in verschiedenen Ausführungen
Les papillons exécutés de différentes manières

12a Shawl of dark-green 'Pagoda' silk
and silk No. 200/6 in several shades of
yellow and pink.

12a Schal aus dunklegrüner 'Pagoda' Seide und
Seide Nm 200/6 in verschiedenen gelb und rosa
Tönen.

12a Châle en soie 'Pagoda' vert foncé et soie
Nm 200/6 en plusieurs tons de jaune et rose.

12a

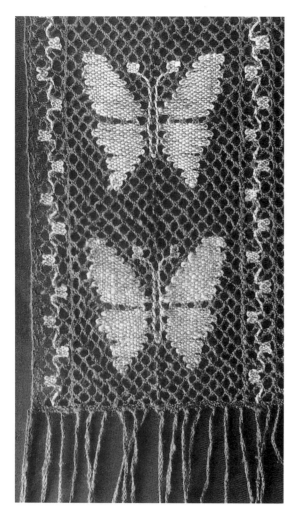

13 Snowflake

A small motif which can be used on its own or in a group. The bars are worked or dropped as required.

4 pairs, linen 40/3, 35/2 or silver thread, dtex 330(1) Gütermann or dtex 350 MEZ Reflecta

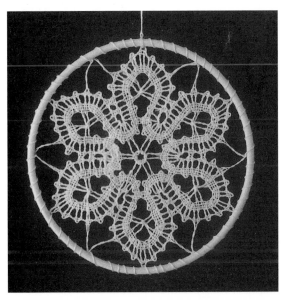

13 Schneeflocke

Ein kleines Motiv, das einzeln oder in einer Gruppe verwendet werden kann. Die Stege werden nach Bedarf ausgeführt oder weggelassen.

4 Paare, Leinen 40/3, 35/2 oder Silberfaden, dtex 330(1) Gütermann oder dtex 350 MEZ Reflecta

13 Le Flocon de neige

Un petit motif qui peut être utilisé individuellement ou en groupe. Suivant les besoins les brides sont exécutées ou omises.

4 paires, lin 40/3, 35/5 ou fil argenté, dtex 330(1) Gütermann ou dtex 350 MEZ Reflecta

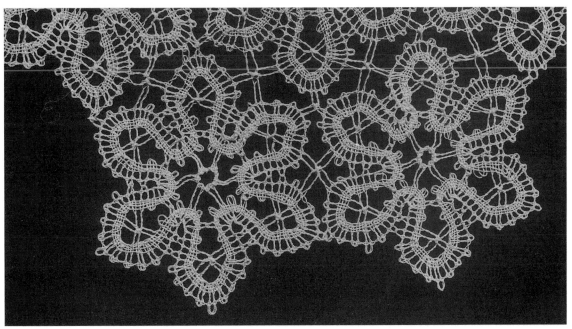

13a The seven snowflakes were made by Ruth Märky. For linen thread 100/3 the pricking was reduced to 66%.

13a Die sieben Schneeflocken hat Ruth Märky geklöppelt. Für den Leinenfaden 100/3 wurde der Klöppelbrief auf 66% reduziert.

13a Les sept flocons de neige sont faits par Ruth Märky. Pour le fil de lin 100/3 le modèle a du être réduit à 66%.

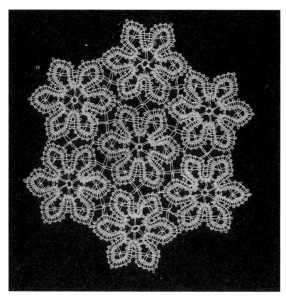

13a

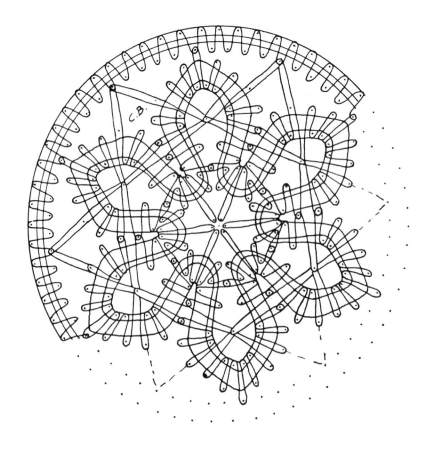

14 Large Bird

The size of the bird must be adapted to the size of the thread. The original bird was made on an A3-sized pricking (141%) with six pairs of thick silver thread (Ophir/MEZ). The choice of fillings is at the discretion of the lacemaker.

14 Grosser Vogel

Die Grösse des Vogels wird der Fadenstärke angepasst. Im Original wurde der Vogel auf einem Klöppelbrief in Format A3 (141%) mit sechs Paar Klöppel mit dickem Silberfaden (Ophir/MEZ) gearbeitet. Die Fläche kann nach eigenen Ideen ausgefüllt werden.

14 Le Grand Oiseau

La grandeur de l'oiseau doit être adaptée à grosseur du fil. L'original a été exécuté sur une piquée du format A3 (141%) en utilisant six paires de gros fil argenté (Ophir/MEZ). Le remplissage peut être exécuté au gré de la dentellière.

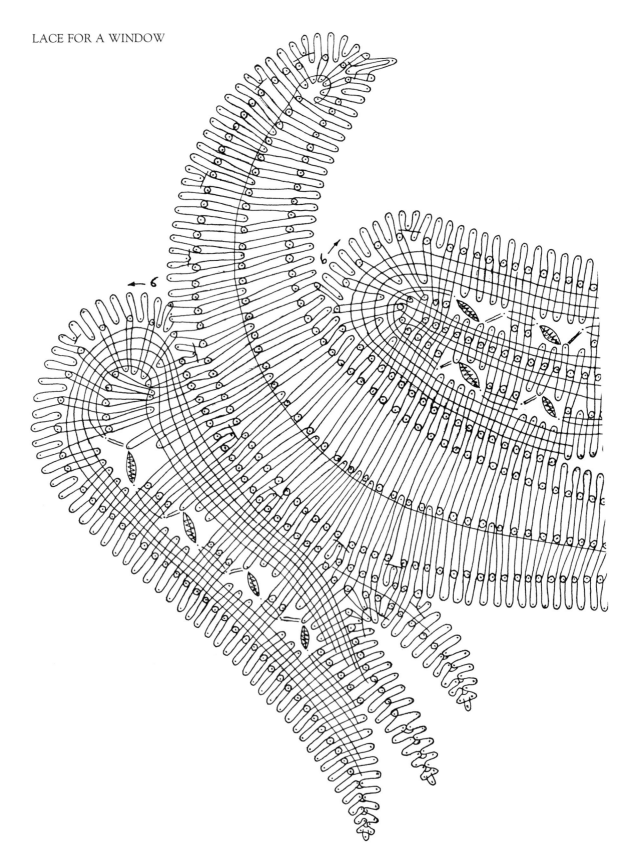

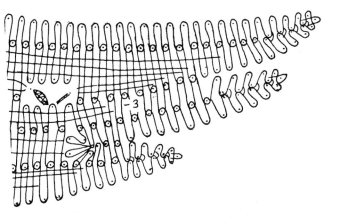

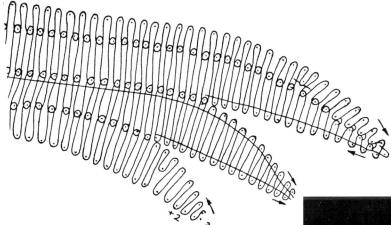

14a

14a The same outline but different stitches: Judith Culatti made her own design in A4 size for linen 60/3.

14a Die gleiche Form, aber eine andere Ausführung: Judith Culatti hat nach ihrem eigenen Entwurf in Format A4 gearbeitet mit Leinen 60/3.

14a La même silhouette, mais des point différents: Judith Culatti a fait son propre dessin en format A4 pour du lin 60/3.

A 5

14a

15 Fishes

The fish is formed by a simple tape in clothstitch and halfstitch. For the 'worker' a thick silver thread was used; for the 'passives' several shades of blue linen were chosen.

5 pairs, linen 35/2 and thick silver thread (MEZ Ophir)

15 Fische

Der Fisch wird durch ein einfaches Band in Leinen- und Halbschlag geformt. Für das Laufpaar wurde dicker Silberfaden verwendet, für die passiven Paare wurde blaues Leinen in verschiedenen Tönen gewählt.

5 Paare, Leinen 35/2 und dicker Silberfaden (MEZ Ophir)

15 Les Poissons

Le poisson est formé par un lacet en mat et en demi-point. Pour le voyageur du gros fil argenté a été utilisé, pour les paires passives du fil de lin bleu en differents tons a été choisi.

5 paires, lin 35/2 et gros fil argenté (MEZ Ophir)

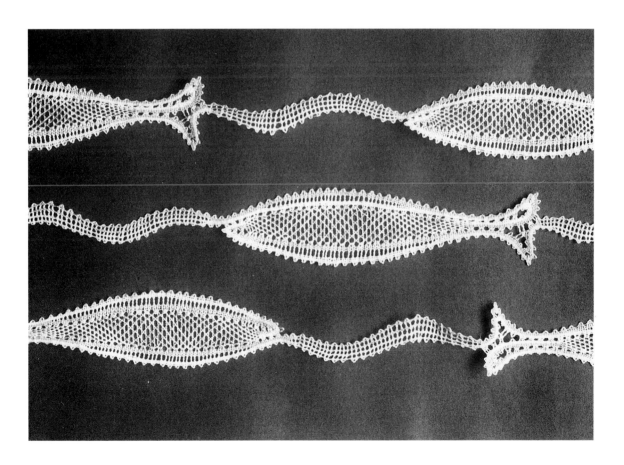

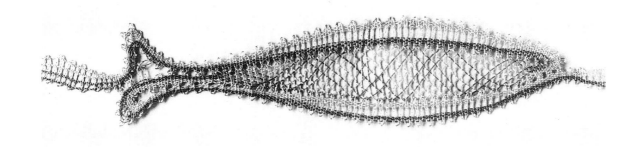

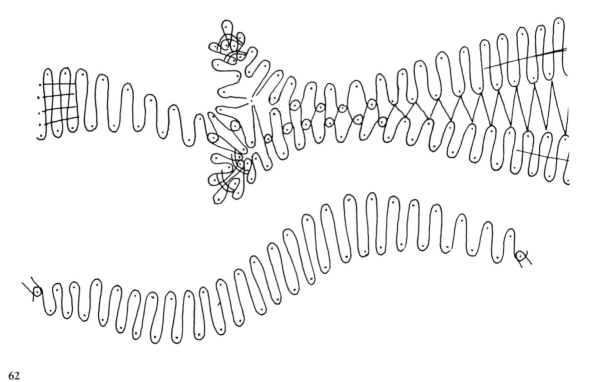

16 Dragonfly

The pinholes between the wings are used twice; the last three are used for sewings joining the upper and lower wing. For more stability the wings can also be joined completely.

7 pairs for each wing.
16a Linen 35/2 and silver thread (to match fish pattern No. 15)
16b Linen 60/2 or 100/3

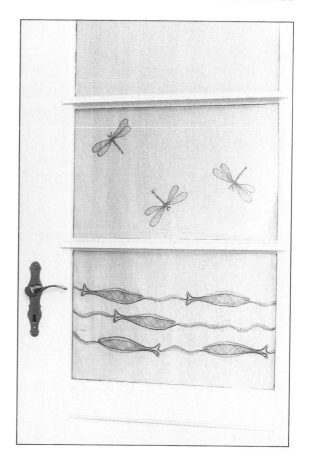

16 Libelle

Die Nadelpunkte zwischen den Flügeln werden zweimal verwendet, bei den letzten drei werden der obere und der untere Flügel mit dem Häklein zusammengehängt. Für besseren Halt können die Flügel auch ganz verbunden werden.

7 Paare pro Flügel.
16a Leinen 35/2 und Silberfaden (passend zum Fischmuster Nr. 15)
16b Leinen 60/2 oder 100/3

16 La Libellule

Les épingles entre les ailes ont été utilisées deux fois, aux trois dernières des points de raccroc fixent l'aile supérieure à l'aile inférieure. Pour plus de stabilité, les ailes peuvent être jointes complètement.

7 paires par ailes.
16a lin 35/3 et fil argenté (correspondant au poisson modèle no 15)
16b lin 60/2 ou 100/3

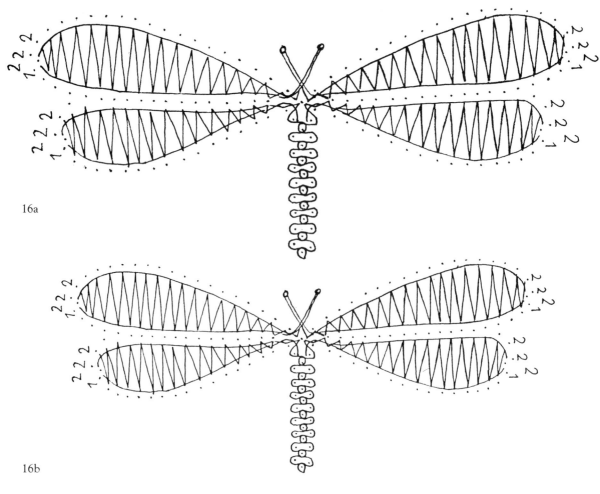

16a

16b

17 Sparrows

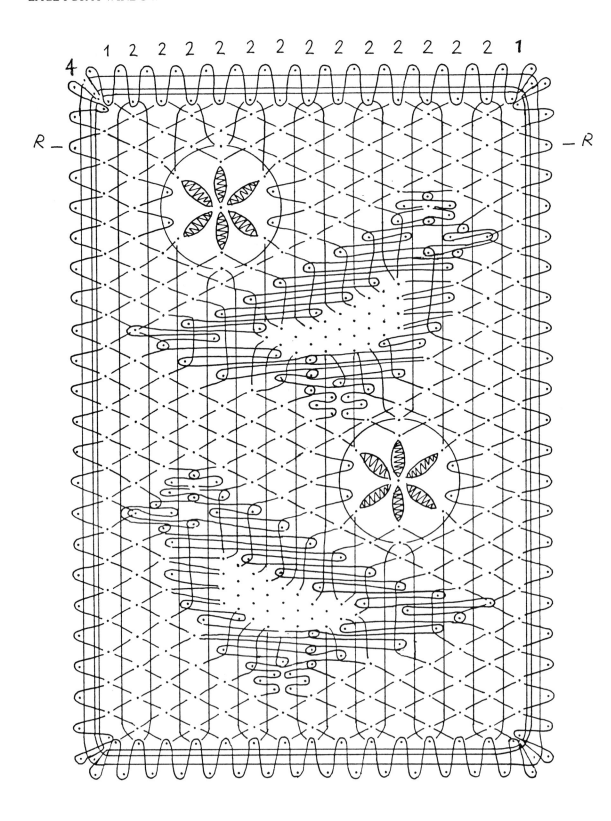

The large curtain shown on p. 49 features a combination of patterns 11 and 17, and was worked by Silvia Huber. The 'seam' at both ends consists of a large piece of clothstitch tape which was made separately.

28 pairs, linen 40/3
Border: 4 pairs, linen 40/3

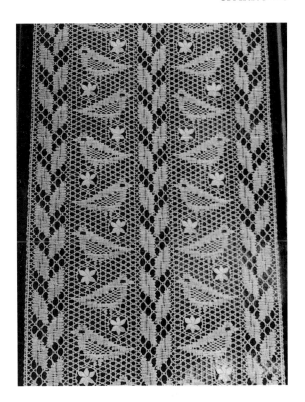

17 Spatzen

Der grosse Vorhang auf Seite 49 wurde von Silvia Huber geklöppelt. Der 'Saum' an beiden Enden besteht aus einem breiten Band in Leinenschlag, das separat hergestellt wurde.

28 Paare, Leinen 40/3
Umrandung: 4 Paare, Leinen 40/3

17 Les Moineaux

Le grand rideau à la page 49 a été confectionné par Silvia Huber. Pour 'l'ourlet' aux deux bouts un ruban large en mat a été fait séparément.

28 paires, lin 40/3
Bordure: 4 paires, lin 40/3

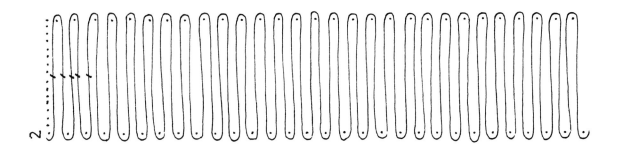

18 X-Pattern

In order to obtain neat edges on both
ends, the starting point for this insertion
is located in the middle of the right-
hand side. The lace is worked round the
corner and the second half is joined
accordingly. (See also pattern 25, pp.
86–7.)

18a Insertion: 15–16 pairs, linen 60/3,
pricking 100%
18b Curtain: 15–16 pairs, linen 40/3,
pricking 118%

18 X-Muster

Um an beiden Enden eine saubere Kante zu
erhalten, befindet sich der Anfang dieses
Entredeux in der Mitte der rechten Hälfte. Die
Spitze wird um die Ecke gearbeitet und die
zweite Hälfte wird entsprechend eingehängt.
(Siehe auch Muster Nr. 25, auf Seiten 86–7.)

18a Entredeux: 15–16 Paare, Leinen 60/3,
Klöppelbrief 100%
18b Vorhang: 15–16 Paare, Leinen 40/3,
Klöppelbreif 118%

18 Modèle en X

Afin d'obtenir un bord net aux deux bouts de
cet entredeux, le commencement se trouve au
milieu de la moitié de droite. Après avoir
travaillé les deux angles, la seconde moitié est
jointe à la partie correspondante. (Voir aussi
modèle no 25 aux pages 86–7.)

18a Entredeux: 15–16 paires, lin 60/3, piquée
100%
18b Rideaux: 15–16 paires, lin 40/3, piquée
118%

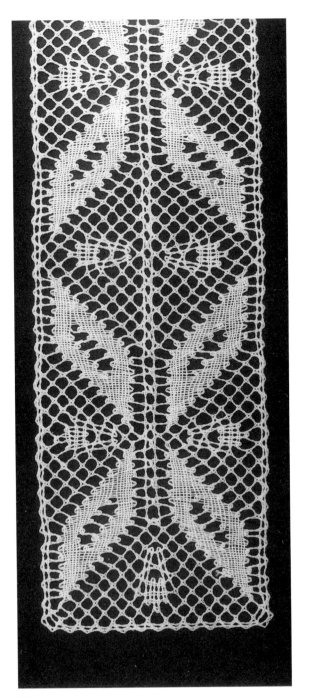

18a

18b

19 Lily

This pattern is worked in alternating
directions, a method which gives a deep
flounce without requiring a large
number of bobbins. For the complete
circle an auxiliary pair of bobbins may
be necessary in order to obtain a neat
centre.

16 pairs, linen 60/3

19 Lilie

Bei diesem Muster wechselt die Arbeitsrichtung
fortwährend. Mit dieser Methode lassen sich
breite Bänder mit einer handlichen Anzahl
Klöppel herstellen. Für den geschlossenen Kreis,
kann ein Hilfspaar nötig sein, um einen schönen
Mittelpunkt zu erhalten.

16 Paare, Leinen 60/3

19 La Fleur de lis

Ce modèle est exécuté en alternant la direction
de travail, une méthode qui permet de faire une
dentelle large en utilisant un nombre de fuseaux
facile à manier. Pour le cercle complet une paire
auxiliaire aide à d'obtenir un centre parfait.

16 paires, lin 60/3

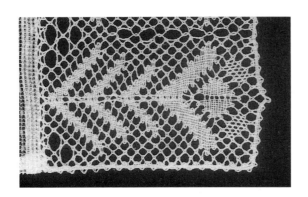

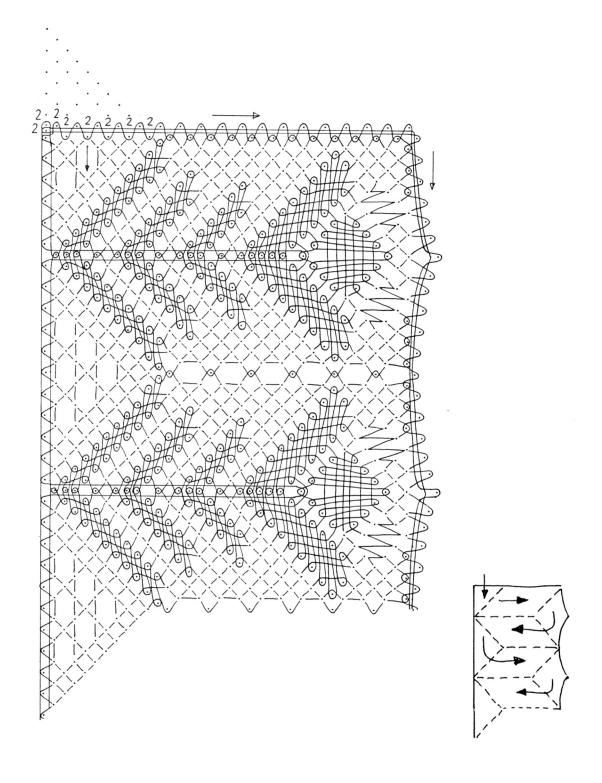

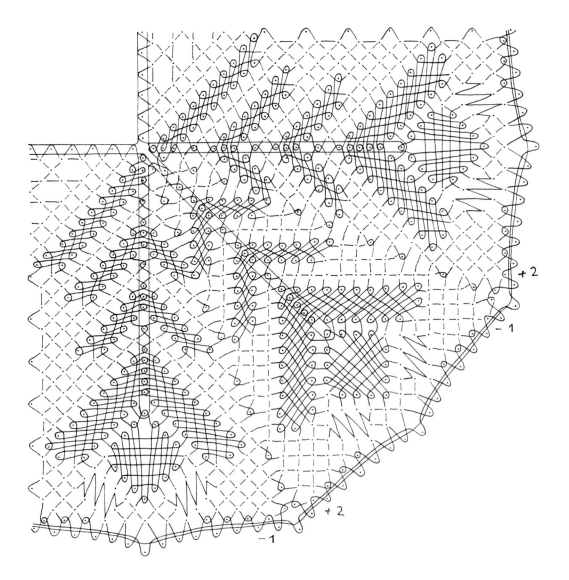

+ 2

- 1

+ 2

- 1

19a/b The lace in a ring is made by
Dora Wyser, the oval version is worked
by Evelyne Lütolf.

19a/b Die Spitze im Ring hat Dora Wyser
geklöppelt, die ovale Variante ist von Evelyne
Lütolf ausgeführt worden.

19a/b La dentelle fixée dans un cercle a été faite
par Dora Wyser, la variante ovale a été exécutée
par Evelyne Lütolf.

19a

19b

20 Small Sun

The bars on the outer side should be
omitted, and a supplementary edge pair
may be added, if the sun is to be
inserted or appliquéd.

Outer edge: 9 pairs, linen 60/3
Centre section: 6 pairs, linen 60/3

20 Kleine Sonne

Die Stege auf der Aussenseite werden
weggelassen und ein zusätzliches Randpaar kann
angefügt werden, falls die Sonne ein- oder
aufgenäht werden soll.

Äusserer Ring: 9 Paare, Leinen 60/3
Zentrum: 6 paare, Leinen 60/3

20 Le Petit Soleil

Les brides du bord extérieur sont omises et une
paire supplémentaire peut être ajoutée en
bordure si le soleil doit être incrusté ou
appliqué.

Partie extérieure: 9 paires, lin 60/3
Centre: 6 paires, lin 60/3

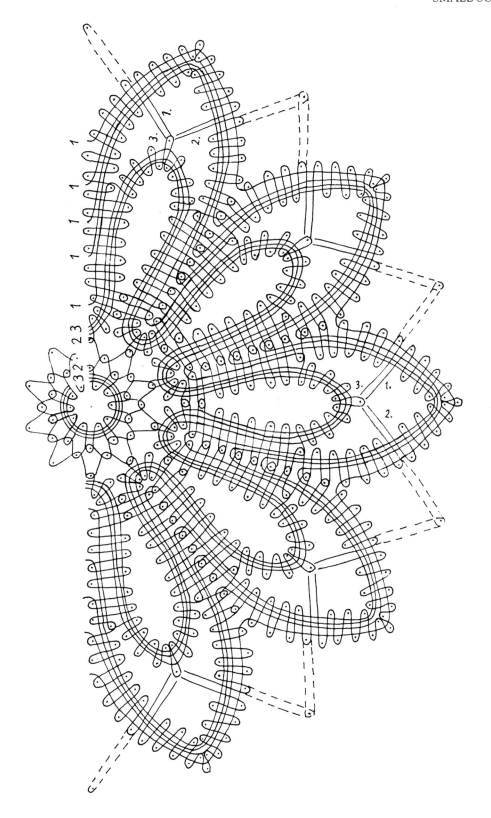

20a Pattern No. 20 (Small Sun) is here combined with Pattern No. 21 (Large Sun) and mounted in a ring with a diameter of 40cm. (approx. 16″).

20a Muster Nr. 20 (Kleine Sonne) und Nr. 21 (Grosse Sonne) in einem Ring von 40cm Durchmesser.

20a Modèle no 20 (Petit Soleil) et no 21 (Grand Soleil) dans un cercle de 40 cm de diamètre.

20a

LACE FOR A
TABLE

SPITZEN FÜR EINEN TISCH
DENTELLE POUR UNE TABLE

21 Large Sun

This edging was made with nine pairs of bobbins, first the twenty repeats of clothstitch tape, then the halfstitch foot. It is, however, possible to work both parts simultaneously with two sets of bobbins. As shown on p. 76 this pattern can be combined with pattern No. 20.

9 pairs, linen 60/3

21 Grosse Sonne

Diese Umrandung wurde mit neun Klöppelpaaren hergestellt, zuerst die zwanzig Rapporte des Leinenschlagbandes, dann den Halbschlagfuss, aber es ist auch möglich, beide Teile gleichzeitig zu machen, mit der doppelten Anzahl Klöppel. Wie auf Seite 76 abgebildet, kann dieses Muster mit Nr. 20 kombiniert werden.

9 Paare, Leinen 60/3

21 Le Grand Soleil

Cette bordure a été exécutée avec neuf paires de fuseaux, d'abord les 20 rapports du lacet en mat, en suite le pied en demi-point, mais il est aussi possible de faire les deux parties simultanément en utilisant la double quantité de fuseaux. Ce modèle peut être combiner avec le no 20 selon l'illustration de la page 76.

9 paires, lin 60/3

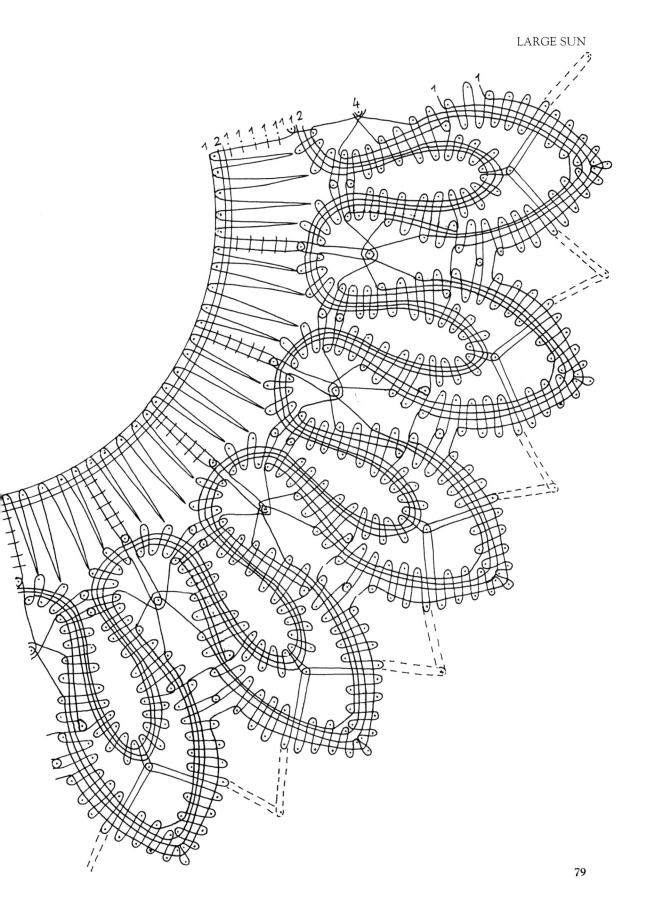

LARGE SUN

79

22 Large Star

Six pairs of bobbins were used for the base, with five pairs for the twelve points. The two tapes may be worked one after the other or simultaneously. A version with eight points is shown on the following pages.

11 pairs, linen 40/3

22 Grosser Stern

Sechs Klöppelpaare als Basis, fünf Paare für die zwölf Zacken, zwei Bänder, die nacheinander oder gleichzeitig gearbeitet werden können. Eine Version mit acht Zacken befindet sich auf den folgenden Seiten.

11 Paare, Leinen 40/3

22 La Grande Etoile

Six paires de fuseaux comme base, cinq paires pour les douze pointes, deux lacets à travailler l'un après l'autre ou simultanément. Une version à huit pointes se trouve aux pages suivantes.

11 paires, lin 40/3

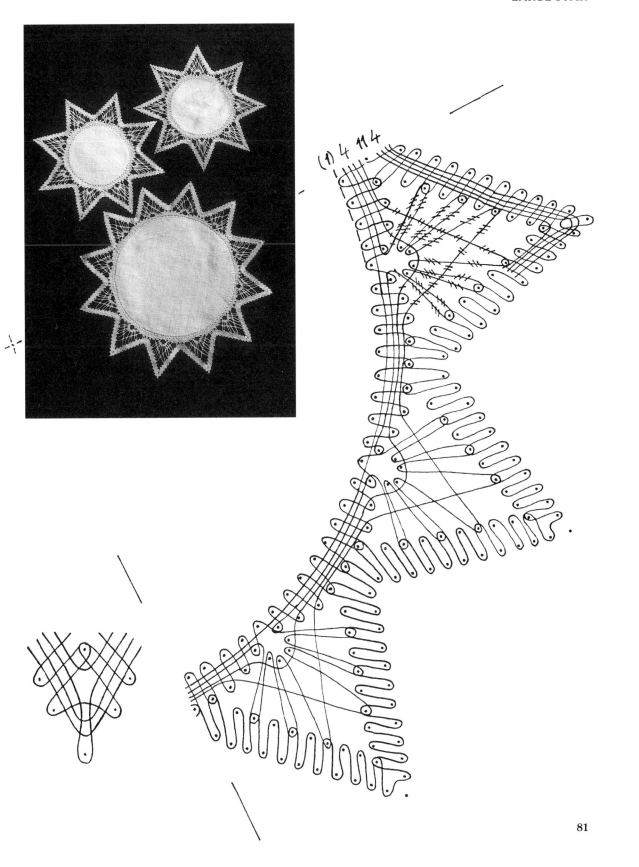

23 Small Star

Basically the same arrangement as for the previous pattern, but with an additional lace centre. The version all in lace, used as a Christmas decoration, is sewn onto a piece of acetate such as that used with overhead projectors.

10–11 pairs for the star, linen 40/3
9 pairs for the centre

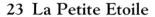

23 Kleiner Stern

Im Prinzip die gleiche Anordnung wie das vorhergehende Muster, aber mit einem zusätzlichen Zentrum aus Spitze. Die ganz geklöppelte Variante, als Weihnachtsdekoration verwendbar, ist auf einer Azetat-Folie (für Hellraumprojektor) aufgenäht.

10–11 Paare für den Stern, Leinen 40/3
9 Paare für das Zentrum

23 La Petite Etoile

En principe le même procédé que le modèle précédant, mais en plus un centre en dentelle. La variante toute en dentelle, servant de décoration de Noël, est cousu sur une feuille d'acétate (pour rétroprojecteur).

10–11 paires pour l'étoile, lin 40/3
9 paires pour le centre

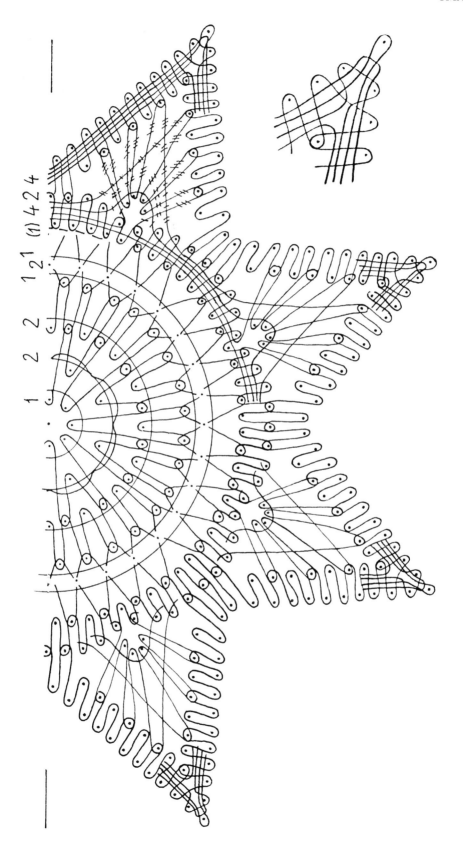

24 Zigzag

The shiny outline is achieved by using a pair of bobbins on either side of machine-plaited gold tape. However, the clothstitch edge can also be worked in the usual way with several passive pairs.

10–16 pairs, linen 35/2
Six pairs can be replaced by two pairs with tape (MEZ Diadem).

24 Zickzack

Die glänzende Umrandung entstand durch je einem Paar Klöppel mit einem maschinell geflochtenem Band, aber der Leinschlagrand kann auch in der üblichen Weise, mit mehreren passiven Paaren, ausgeführt werden.

10–16 Paare, Leinen 35/2
Sechs Paare können mit zwei Paaren mit Band (MEZ Diadem) ersetzt werden.

24 Zigzag

Le bord brillant de chaque côté est formé par une paire de fuseaux garni d'un lacet tressé mécaniquement, mais le bord en mat peut aussi être fait de manière conventionelle en utilisant plusieurs paires passives.

10–16 paires, lin 35/2
Six paires peuvent être remplacées par deux paires de lacet (MEZ Diadem).

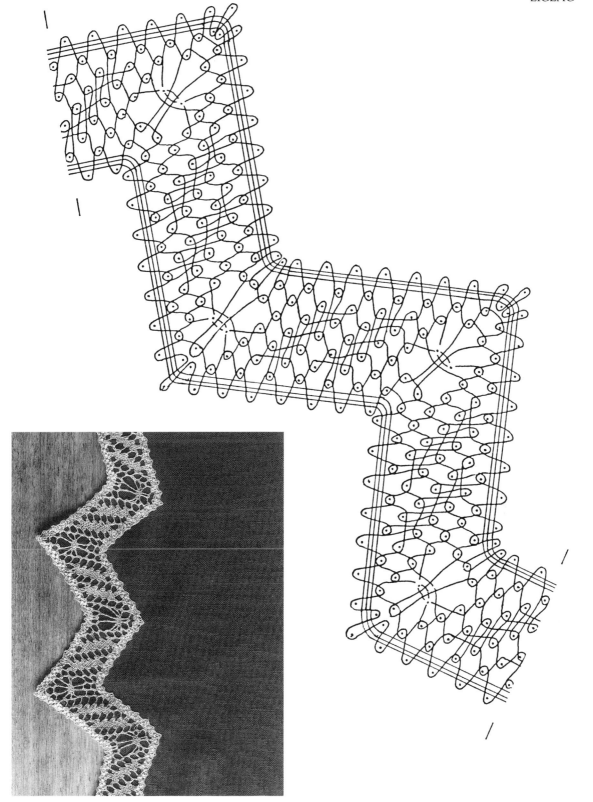

25 Tulips

This edging can be mounted along the edge of a large square or rectangular tablecloth. However, it can also be used for a small mat all in lace in combination with pattern No. 18, providing the clothstitch foot is dropped. The version all in lace was worked by Orsina Dübendorfer.

16 pairs, linen 60/3

25 Tulpen

Diese Spitze kann als Randverzierung eines grossen, quadratischen oder rechteckigen Tischtuches verwendet werden. Aber auch ein Läufer ganz aus Spitze lässt sich herstellen, zusammen mit Muster Nr. 18, wobei der Leinenschlagrand wegfällt. Die Version ganz aus Spitze wurde von Orsina Dübendorfer geklöppelt.

16 Paare, Leinen 60/3

25 Les Tulipes

Ce modèle peut être utilisé pour orner le bord d'une grande nappe carrée ou rectangulaire. Mais il est aussi possible de faire un tapis de table tout en dentelle en conjonction avec le no 18, à condition d'omettre le pied en mat. La version tout en dentelle a été exécutée par Orsina Dübendorfer.

16 paires, lin 60/3

25a Tulips and X-Pattern
   Tulpen und X-Muster
   Les tulipes et modèle en X

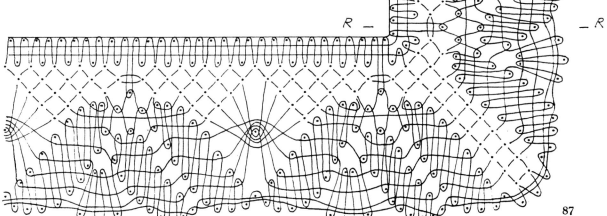

87

26 Large Rhombus

This broad pattern can be worked in
two sections, the second half being
attached with sewings. A separate tape is
made to hide the knotted thread ends.
The length of the serviette rings must be
adapted to the size of the serviettes.
Instead of knotting the lace into a ring,
both ends can be pinned together with a
toothpick.

46 (or 2 × 23) pairs, linen 35/2 (serviette
rings: 22 pairs)

26 Grosser Rhombus

Dieses breite Muster kann in zwei Teilen
gearbeitet werden, die zweite Hälfte wird
angehäkelt. Ein separates Band deckt die
verknoteten Fadenenden zu. Die Länge der
Serviettenringe muss der Grösse der Servietten
angepasst werden. Statt die Spitze zum Ring zu
verknoten, können beide Ende mit einem
Zahnstocher zusammengehalten werden.

46 (oder 2 × 23) Paare, Leinen 35/2
(Serviettenringe: 22 Paare)

26 Le Grand Losange

Ce modèle large peut être fait en deux parties, la
seconde moitié étant jointe par des points de
raccroc. Un lacet séparé recouvre les noeuds de
la fin. La longeur des liens de serviette doit être
adaptée aux serviettes. Au lieu de nouer la
dentelle en rond il est possible de fixer les deux
bouts par un cure-dent.

46 (ou 2 × 23) paires, lin 35/3 (liens de serviette:
22 paires)

1 2 2 2 2 2 2 2 2 2 2 2 2 2 2 2 2 2 2 2 2 2 1

R —   — *R*

R —   — *R*

2   2   2   2   2   2   2   2   ← 6

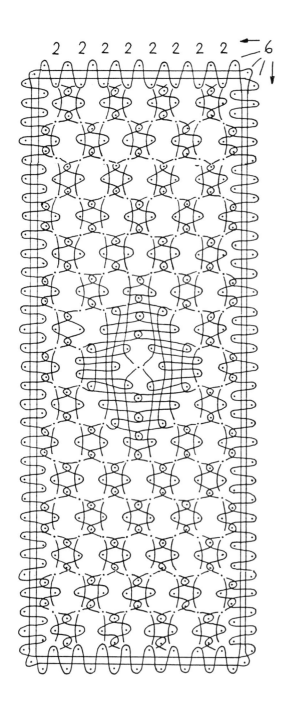

26a Marty Würgler made this large strip of blue lace, which is exactly the length of her dining table.

26a Marty Würgler hat diese breite, blaue Spitze geklöppelt, die genau so lang ist wie ihr Esszimmertisch.

26a Marty Würgler a fait cette large dentelle bleu qui a exactement la longueur de sa table de salle à manger.

26a

27 Large Spiders

The mats and the lampshade are worked
to and fro. The top of the lampshade is
trimmed with separately made halfstitch
tape. The lampshade was made by Silvia
Zwicky, the mat with twelve sections by
Margrit Ebner, the round mat by Dora
Wyser.

14 pairs, linen 40/3
Lampshade: diameter 40 cm., height
23 cm.

---

27 Grosse Spinnen

Sowohl die Decke, als auch der Lampenschirm
werden hin und her gearbeitet. Um den oberen
Rand des Lampenschirmes einzufassen, wurde
ein Band in Halbschlag separat hergestellt. Den
Lampenschirm hat Silvia Zwicky angefertigt, die
zwölfeckige Decke Margrit Ebner, die runde
Decke Dora Wyser.

14 Paare, Leinen 40/3
Lampenschirm: Durchmesser 40 cm., Höhe 23
cm.

---

27 Les Grandes Araignées

Le napperon ainsi que l'abat-jour sont travaillé
en allant et venant. Le haut de l'abat-jour est
bordé d'un lacet en demi-point exécuté
séparément. L'abat-jour a été confectionné par
Silvia Zwicky, le napperon à douze angles par
Margrit Ebner, le napperon rond par Dora
Wyser.

14 paires, lin 40/3
L'Abat-jour: diamètre 40 cm., hauteur 23 cm.

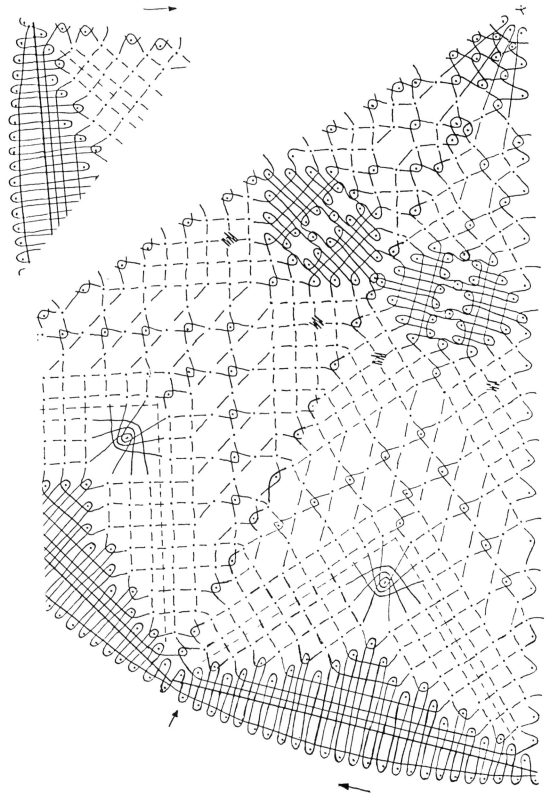

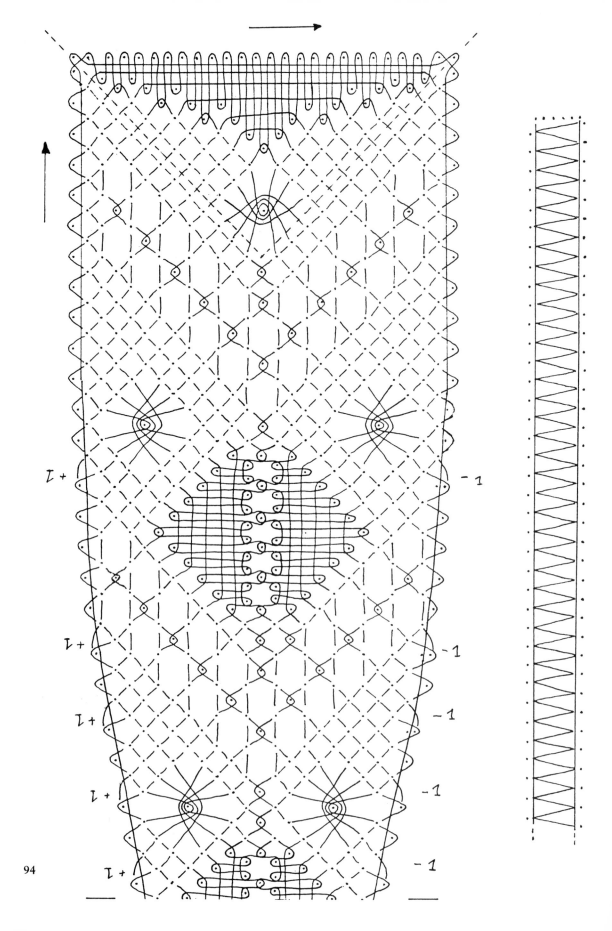

94

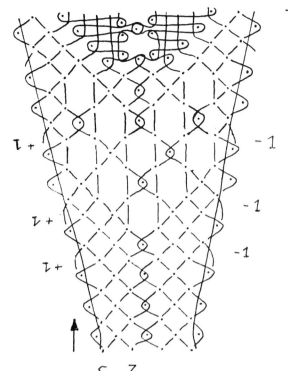

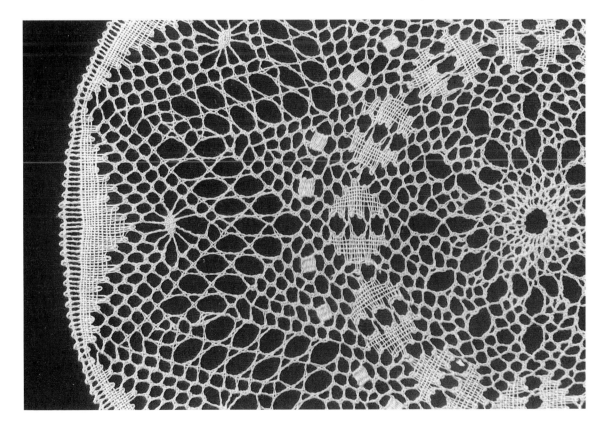

28 Bow Edging

This straight lace is flexible enough to fit around a large circular tablecloth. Three different corners for rectangular tablecloths or serviettes are included.

28a Tablecloth and serviettes: 10 pairs, linen 40/2 or 35/2

28b Handkerchief: linen 80/3 or silk No. 70/3

28 Bogenkante

Diese gerade Spitze ist biegsam und passt auch um ein grosses, rundes Tischtuch. Drei verschiedene Ecken gehören dazu, für rechteckige Tischtücher oder für Servietten.

28a Tischtuch und Servietten: 10 Paare Leinen 40/2 oder 35/2

28b Taschentuch: Leinen 80/3 oder Seide Nr. 70/3

28 Le Bordure à festons

Cette dentelle droite est assez flexible pour s'adapter à une grande nappe ronde. Les trois angles différents sont prévus pour des nappes rectangulaires ou des serviettes.

28a Nappe et Serviettes: 10 paires lin 40/2 ou 35/2

28b Mouchoir: lin 80/3 ou soie No 70/3

28a

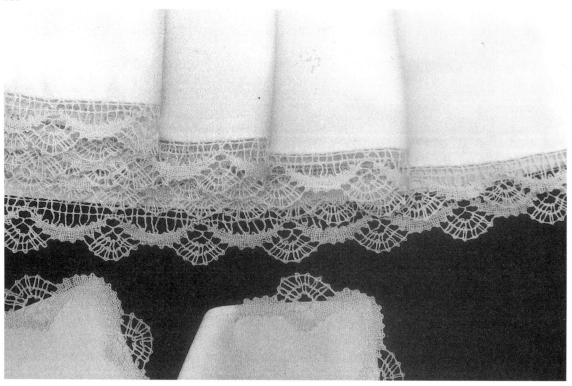

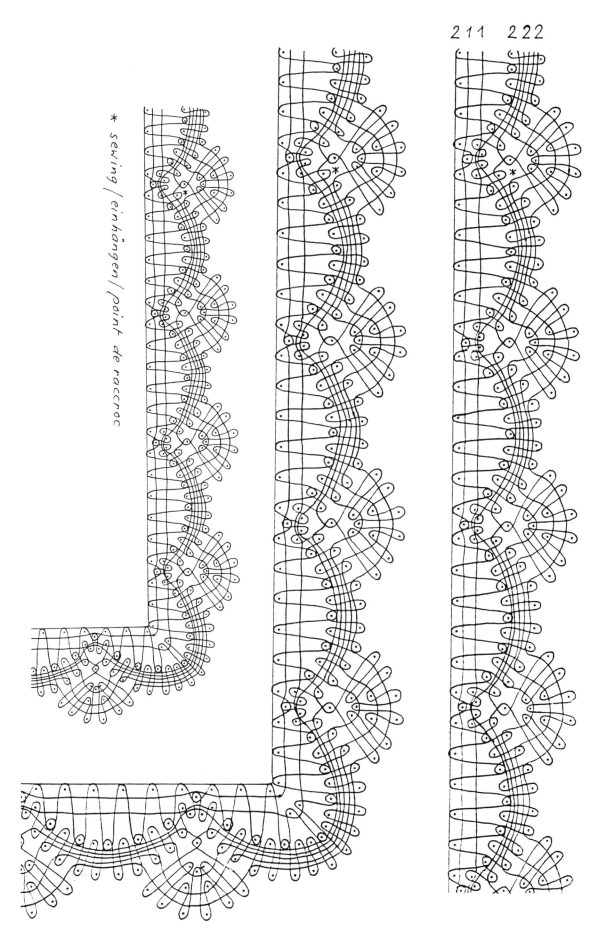

2 1 1   2 2 2

* sewing / einhängen / point de raccroc

The various pieces based on the same pattern were made by three different lacemakers: the white handkerchief with white lace by Theres Schmucki (28b), the yellow tablecloth and serviettes with yellow lace by Yvonne Nüssli (28a, e), the pink mat and serviettes with white lace by Emmy Meier (28c, d).

Die verschiedenen Arbeiten nach dem gleichen Muster wurden von drei verschiedenen Klöpplerinnen ausgeführt: Das weisse Taschentuch mit der weissen Spitze von Theres Schmucki (28b), das gelbe Tischtuch samt Servietten mit gelber Spitze von Yvonne Nüssli (28a, e), das rosa Platzdeckchen samt Servietten mit weisser Spitze von Emmy Meier (28c, d).

Les divers ouvrages d'après le même modèle ont été confectionnés par trois dentellières différentes: le mouchoir blanc à dentelle blanche de Theres Schmucki (28b), la nappe et les serviettes jaune à dentelle jaune d'Yvonne Nüssli (28a, e), le napperon et les serviettes roses à dentelle blanche d'Emmy Meier (28c, d).

28b

28c

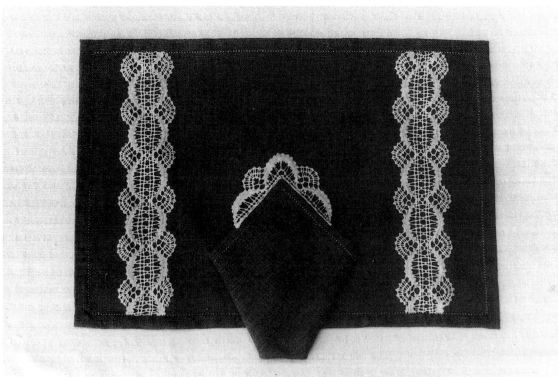

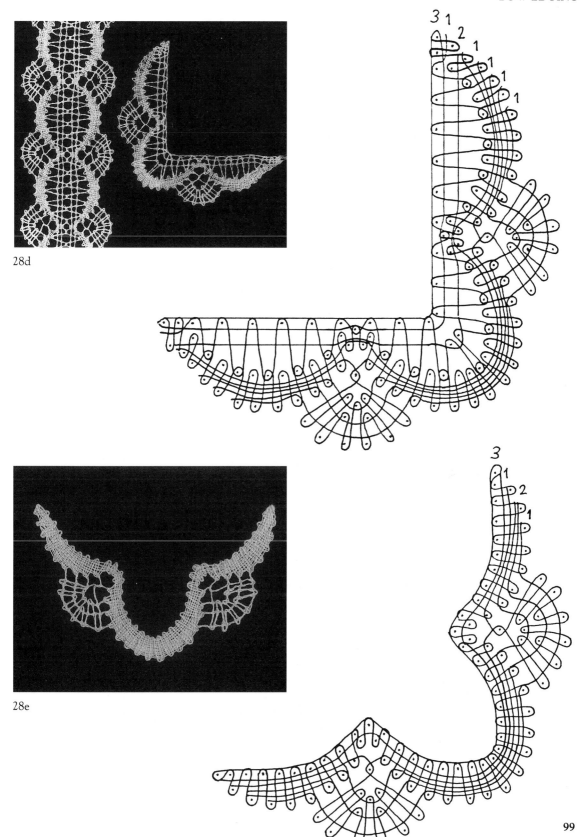

28d

28e

29 Laurel

For a full circle 36 repeats will be necessary, whether the pattern is used in the original size or at a reduced scale.

23 pairs, linen 35/2 and one pair with a gimp
Mat: diameter approx. 56 cm.

29 Lorbeer

Für einen ganzen Kreis braucht es 36 Rapporte, unabhängig davon ob das Muster in Originalgrösse oder verkleinert angewendet wird.

23 Paare, Leinen 35/2 und ein Paar mit Konturfaden
Decke: Durchmesser ca. 56 cm.

29 Le Laurier

Pour un cercle complet il faut confectionner 36 rapports, tant pour le modèle en grandeur originale qu'en format réduit.

23 paires, lin 35/2 et une paire pour le fil de contour
Napperon: diamètre approx. 56 cm.

30 Flowerbuds

As shown by the arrows in the diagram
the two insertions do not really cross
each other. A contrasting colour can be
chosen for the weavers. If the lace is
inserted between two seams, a straight
edge will be convenient, otherwise a
more substantial foot looks better.

2 × 20/22 pairs, linen 35/2 (available in
many shades)
(See also diagram, p. 147)

---

30 Blütenknospen

Wie die Pfeile in der Zeichnung zeigen, kreuzen
sich die zwei Entredeux nur scheinbar. Die
Laufpaare können andersfarbig sein. Wird die
Spitze zwischen zwei Hohlsäumen eingenäht,
genügt ein einfacher, gerader Rand, sonst ist eine
stabilere Umrandung vorteilhafter.

2 × 20/22 Paare, Leinen 35/2 (in vielen Farben
erhältlich)
(Siehe auch Klöppelbrief, Seite 147)

---

30 Les Boutons de fleur

Les flèches dans le dessin montrent que les deux
entredeux ne se croisent pas vraiment. Les deux
voyageurs peuvent être d'une couleur
contrastante. Pour le montage entre deux
ourlets, un bord simple est suffisant, autrement
un pied plus stable est préférable.

2 × 20/22 paires, lin 35/2 (disponible en
plusieurs teintes)
(Voir aussi piquée, page 147)

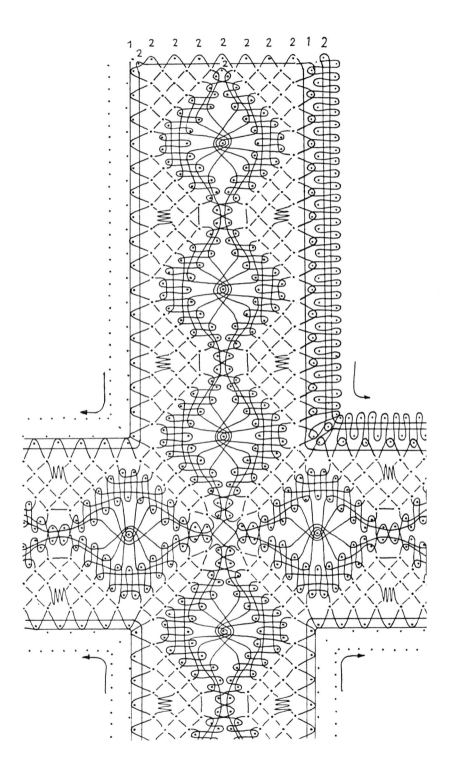

1 2 2 2 2 2 2 2 1 2

31–34 Patchwork

Four different square motifs and two narrow tapes, one for joining the patches, another for the outer edge, are required for constructing covers of any rectangular size.

Squares:
inner part: 6 pairs, linen 60/3
outer part: 5 pairs

Connecting tape and edge tape: 6 pairs each

31–34 Patchwork

Vier verschiedene, quadratische Motive und zwei schmale Bandspitzen, die eine als Verbindung, die andere als Umrandung, das sind die Elemente, um rechteckige Decken in beliebiger Grösse zusammenzustellen.

Quadrate:
innerer Teil: 6 Paare, Leinen 60/3
äusserer Teil: 5 Paare

Verbindung und Umrandung: je 6 Paare

31–34 Patchwork

Quatre motifs carrés différents et deux lacets étroits, l'un pour joindre les pièces, l'autre pour entourer le toute, voilà les éléments pour composer des napperons rectangulaires de toutes les grandeurs.

Carrés:
partie intérieure: 6 paires, lin 60/3
partie extérieure: 5 paires

Jonction ou bordure: 6 paires

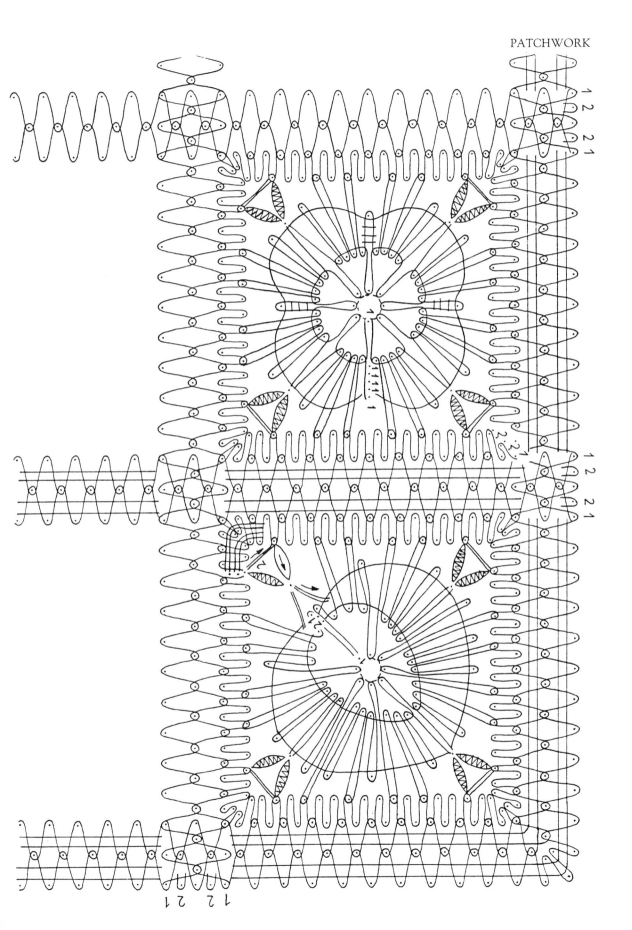

1 2 2 1

1 2 2 1

1 2 2 1

LACE FOR A TABLE

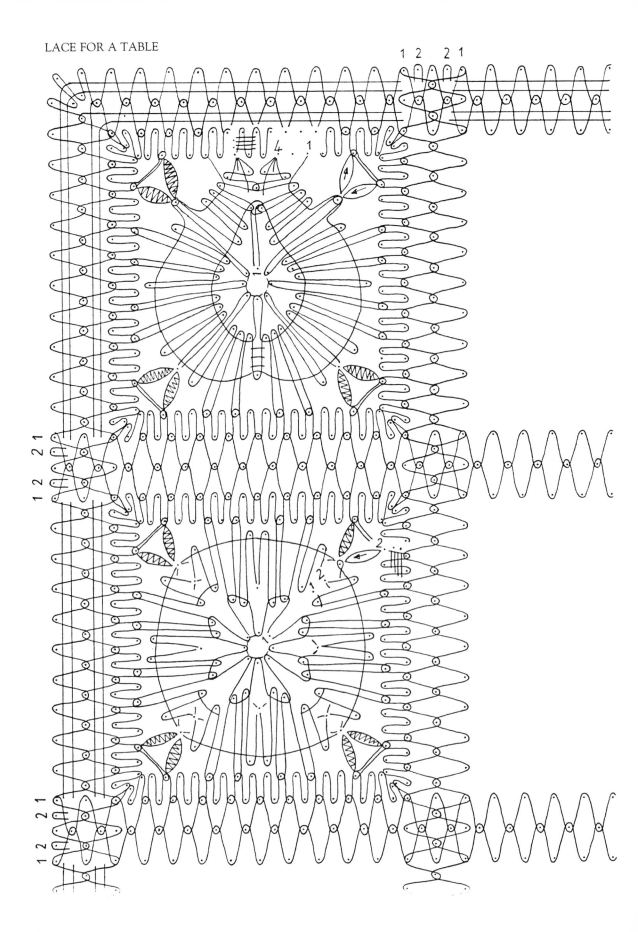

31

32

33

34

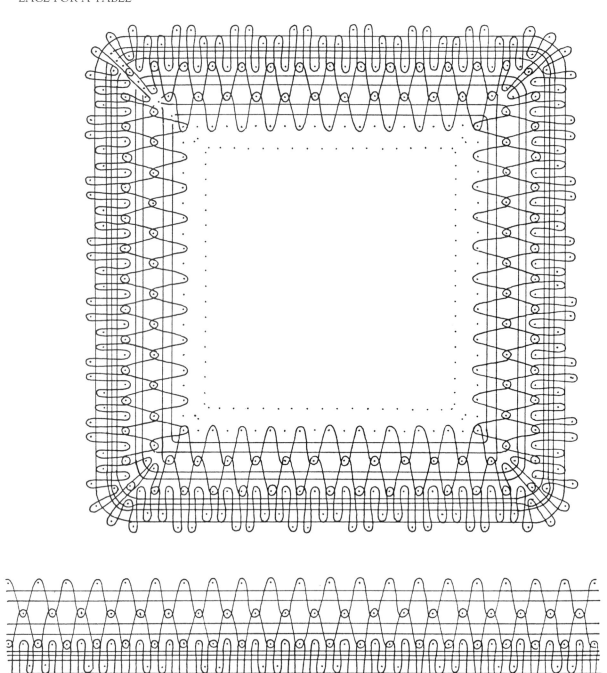

Edging
Umrandung
Bordure

35 Large Triangle

The same tape forms the outer and inner parts of the triangles. These can be arranged in several ways, so that large pieces of various shapes can be worked without interruption.

7–8 pairs, linen 40/3 or 35/2

---

35 Grosses Dreieck

Das gleich Band bildet die äusseren und inneren Teile der Dreiecke, die auf mehrere Arten angeordnet werden können, so dass grosse Gebilde in verschiedenen Formaten ohne Unterbrechung gearbeitet werden können.

7–8 Paare, Leinen 40/3 or 35/2

---

35 Le Grand Triangle

C'est toujours le même lacet qui forme les parties extérieures et intérieures des triangles qui peuvent être disposés de plusieurs manières afin d'obtenir de grandes pièces de différents formats sans interrompre le travail.

7–8 paires, lin 40/3 ou 35/2

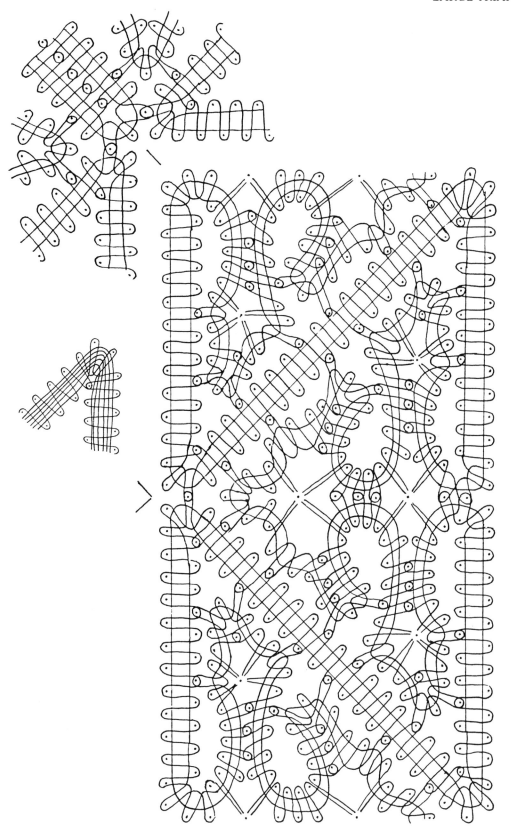

36 Waterlily

The flower is made first, then the green threads for the inner circle of the big leaf are sewn to the flower and worked round. The following rows are attached with 'sewings'.

Flower: centre 5 pairs, petals 5–6 pairs, linen 35/2
Leaf: 10, 10 and 5 pairs, linen 35/2

36 Seerose

Zuerst wird die Blüte geklöppelt, dann werden die grünen Fäden für den inneren Kreis des grossen Blattes an die Blüte gehängt und verarbeitet. Die folgenden Reihen werden mit dem Häklein verbunden.

Blüte: innen 5 Paare, aussen 5–6 Paare, Leinen 35/2
Blatt: 10, 10 und 5 Paare, Leinen 35/2

36 Le Nénuphar

La fleur est faite en premier, puis les fils verts pour le centre de la feuille, sont fixés à la fleur et sont travaillés en rond. Les bandes suivantes sont accrochées par des points de raccroc.

Fleur: centre 5 paires, pétales 5–6 paires, lin 35/2
Feuille: 10, 10 et 5 paires, lin 35/2

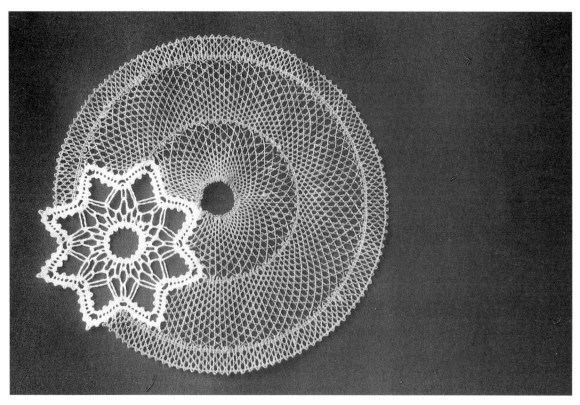

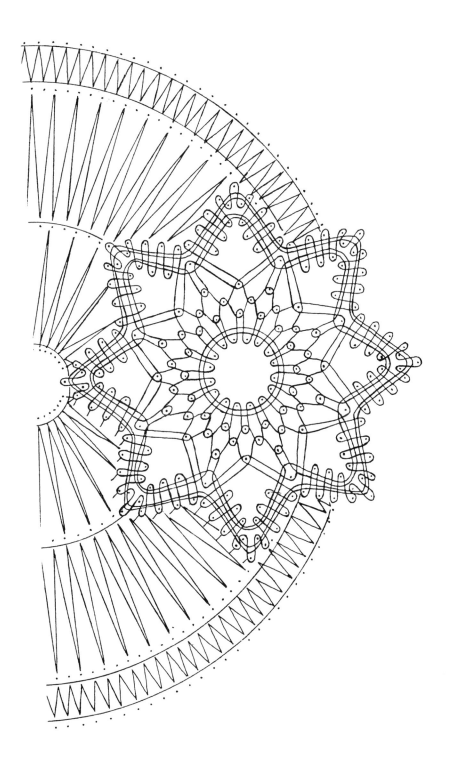

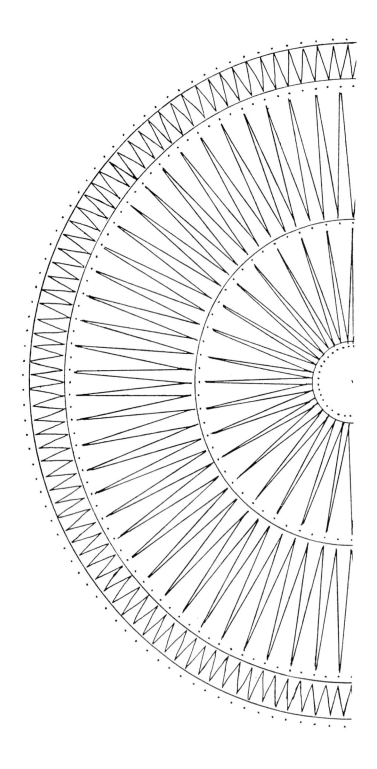

SMALL PRESENTS

KLEINE GESCHENKE
PETITS CADEAUX

37 Hearts

The shape of the heart is always the same, only the connecting parts are different. Twenty repeats of the edging will be necessary for a full circle. The smaller mat all in lace (shown in photograph 37b) was made with linen 60/2 (pricking 85%).

37a Rectangular mat: 9 pairs, linen 60/3
37b Small mat 100%: 7 pairs, linen 60/3 (85% – linen 60/2)
37c Circular border: 7–8 pairs, linen 60/3

37 Herzen

Die Form der Herzen bleibt immer gleich, nur die Verbindungsteile sind verschieden. Zwanzig Rapporte der Einfassung ergeben einen vollen Kreis. Das kleinere Deckchen ganz aus Spitze (siehe Fotografie 37b) wurde mit Leinen 60/2 (Klöppelbrief 85%) hergestellt.

37a Rechteckige Decke: 9 Paare, Leinen 60/3
37b Kleine Decke 100%: 7 Paare, Leinen 60/3 (85% – Leinen 60/2)
37c Kreisförmige Umrandung: 7–8 Paare, Leinen 60/3

37a

37 Les Coeurs

La forme des coeurs est toujours la même, seulement les parties intermédiaires sont différentes. Vingt rapports de la bordure sont nécessaires pour obtenir un cercle complet. Le plus petit napperon tout en dentelle (voir la photographie 37b) a été confectionné avec du lin 60/2 (piquée 85%).

37a Napperon rectangulaire: 9 paires, lin 60/3
37b Napperon rond 100%: 7 paires, lin 60/3 (85% – lin 60/2)
37c Bordure circulaire: 7–8 paires, lin 60/3

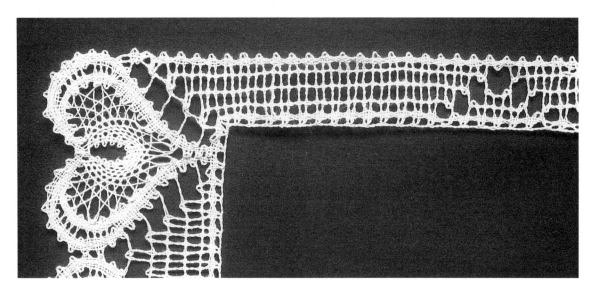

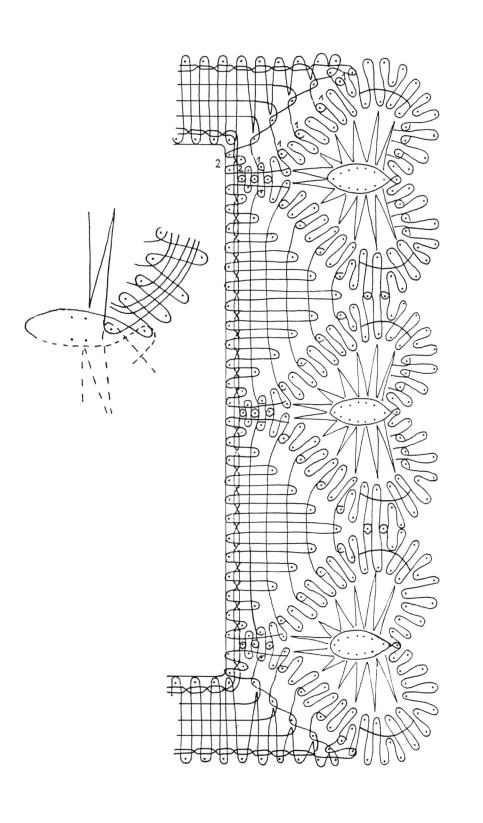

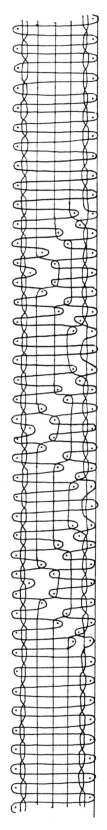

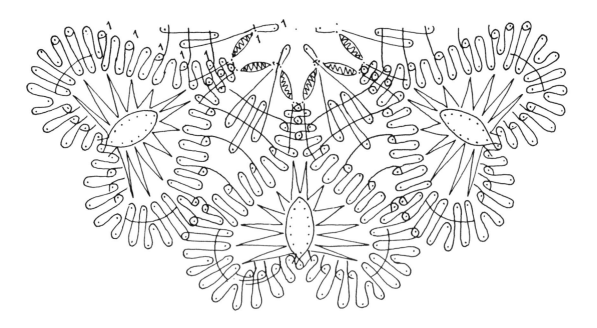

37b

37c

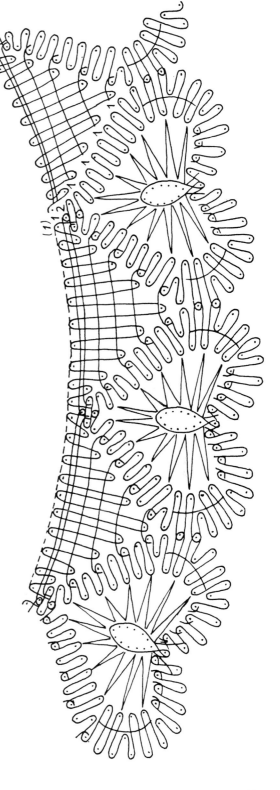

38 Wedding Rings

This triangular motif can be used in many ways. If the lace is to be sewn onto the fabric then the edge pair, the bars and even the 'flower' may be omitted. The eight-sided tablecloth was made by Elvira Bachmann.

6 pairs, linen 35/2, or 7 pairs (octogon), linen 60/3

38 Eheringe

Dieses dreieckige Motiv passt zu vielen Formaten. Falls das Motiv auf den Stoff appliziert wird, können die Stege und sogar die 'Blüte' weggelassen werden. Das achteckige Tischtuch ist von Elvira Bachmann hergestellt worden.

6 Paare, Leinen 35/2, oder 7 Paare (Achteck), Leinen 60/3

38 Les Alliances

Ce motif triangulaire convient à toutes sortes de formats. Au cas ou la dentelle est appliquée sur le tissu, les brides et même la 'fleur' peuvent être omises. La nappe octogonale a été exécutée par Elvira Bachmann.

6 paires, lin 35/2, ou 7 paires (octogone), lin 60/3

Flower made of two motifs
Ansteckblume aus zwei Motiven
Une fleur composée de deux motifs

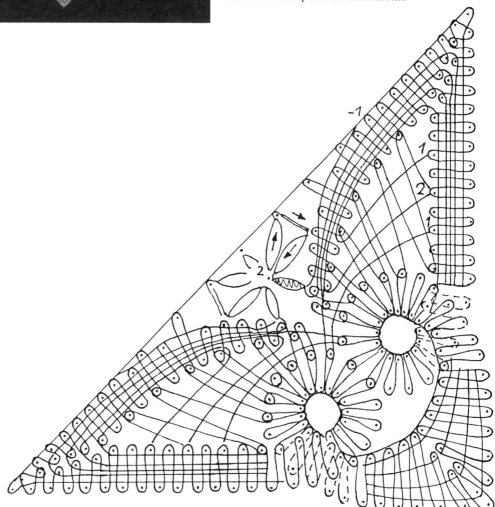

39 Small Spiders

This doll collar can be started in two different ways; the number of bobbins will vary accordingly. The number of repeats must be adapted to the size of the doll. Seven to eight repeats will be enough for cuffs, for a small mat eighteen repeats represent a full circle. (See Pattern 40 for suggested centre.)

13–15 pairs, linen 60/3 (or start with 6 pairs in the middle of the inner circle and add 3 pairs for outer part)

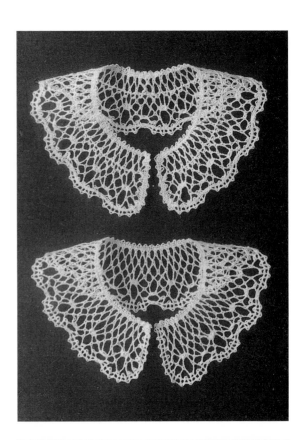

39 Kleine Spinnen

Dieser Puppenkragen kann auf zwei Arten begonnen werden; die Anzahl Klöppel variert entsprechend. Die Anzahl Rapporte muss der Grösse der Puppe angepasst werden. Sieben bis acht Rapporte reichen für Manschetten, für ein Deckchen ergeben achtzehn Wiederholungen einen vollen Kreis. (Für passende Mitte siehe Muster 40.)

13–15 Paare, Leinen 60/3 (oder mit 6 Paaren in der Mitte des inneren Kreises beginnen und für die äussere Hälfte 3 Paare einfügen)

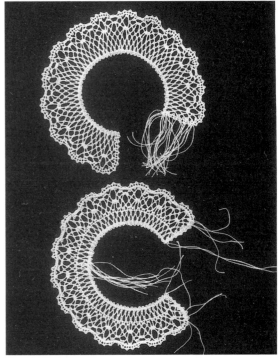

39 Les Petites Araigneés

Ce col de poupée peut être commencé de deux manières; le nombre de fuseaux varie analoguement. Le nombre de rapports doit être adapter à la grandeur de la poupée. Sept à huit rapports suffisent à la confection de manchettes, pour un petit napperon, dix-huit répétitions représentent un cercle complet. (Pour centre sugéré voir modèle 40.)

13–15 paires, lin 60/3 (ou commencer avec 6 paires au milieu de la partie intérieur et ajouter 3 paires pour le bord extérieur)

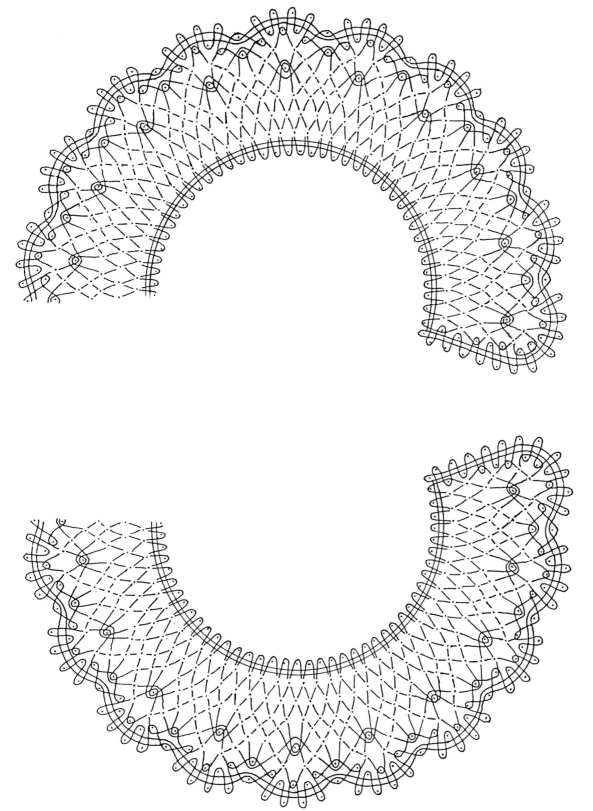

40 Halfstitch Rosette

A mat with a large opening in the middle for the stems of the flowers and with long bars for inserting a ribbon can be used as a frill for a small bouquet. The outer ring can be replaced by pattern No. 39. The inner part (with two additional pairs) can be used in a doll's house – the height of the jug is less than 5 cm. (2 inches).

Outer circle: 10 pairs; centre: 10–12 pairs; linen 60/3

40 Halbschlag Rosette

Ein Deckchen mit einer grossen Oeffnung in der Mitte für die Blumenstiele, dazu lange Stege, um ein Band einzuziehen, das ergibt eine Manschette für einen kleinen Blumenstrauss. Der äussere Ring kann mit Muster 39 ausgetauscht werden. Der innere Teil (mit zwei zusätzlichen Paaren) kann als Deckchen für die Puppenstube dienen – die Höhe des Kruges beträgt knapp 5 cm.

Ring: 10 Paare; Mitte: 10–12 Paare; Leinen 60/3

40 La Rosette en demi-point

Un napperon avec une grande ouverture au centre pour les tiges des fleurs, ainsi que de longues brides pour laisser passer un ruban, celà sert de manchette à un petit bouquet de fleur. Le cercle extérieur peut être remplacé par le modèle no 39. La partie centrale (deux paires en plus) peut servir de napperon pour une chambre de poupée – le cruchon mesure à peine 5 cm. en hauteur.

Cercle: 10 paires; centre: 10–12 paires; lin 60/3

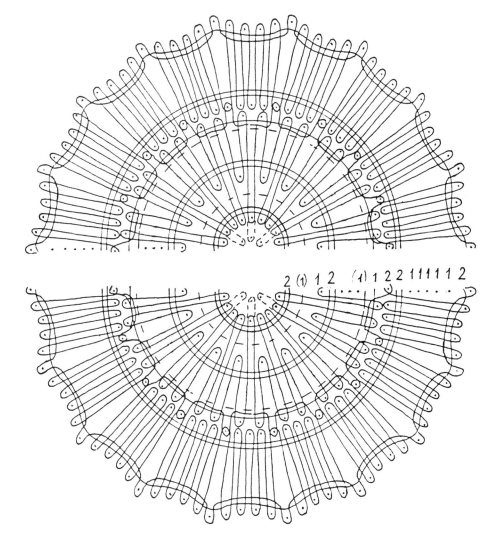

2 (1) 1 2 (1) 1 2 2 1 1 1 1 1 2

41 Dwarfs

These little figures consist of three 'tapes', each in a different colour. For white linen 60/3 the pattern was reduced by 10%.

4/5/5 pairs, linen 35/2 (light and dark green, red)

41 Zwerge

Diese kleinen Figuren bestehen aus drei 'Bändchen', jedes in einer anderen Farbe. Für weisses Leinen 60/3 wurde das Muster um 10% verkleinert.

4/5/5 Paare, Leinen 35/2 (hell- und dunkelgrün, rot)

41 Les Petits Nains

Ces figurines sont formées par trois lacets, chacun d'une couleur différente. Pour le lin blanc 60/3 le modèle a été reduit de 10%.

4/5/5 paires, lin 35/2 (vert clair et foncé, rouge)

42 Foot

Lacemakers sometimes speak a strange language – a lace foot is usually the correct term for the edge of a piece of lace which is next to the fabric. However, the same word may have a completely different meaning, as is demonstrated by this bathmat.

5 pairs, linen 35/2

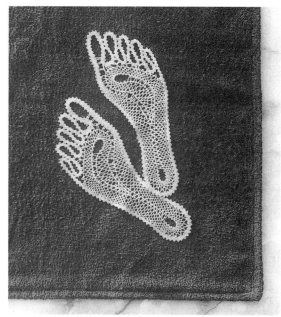

42 Fuss

Klöpplerinnen sprechen manchmal eine seltsame Sprache – ein Spitzenfuss ist die Bezeichnung für die Kante der Spitze, die an den Stoff grenzt. Das gleiche Wort kann jedoch eine ganz andere Bedeutung haben, wie dieser Badteppich zeigt.

5 Paare, Leinen 35/2

42 Le Pied

Les dentellières parlent un langage étrange – un pied de dentelle c'est le terme pour le bord de la dentelle, qui ce trouve le long du tissu. Toutefois, ce mot peut avoir un sens complètement différent, comme le démontre ce tapis de bain.

5 paires, lin 35/2

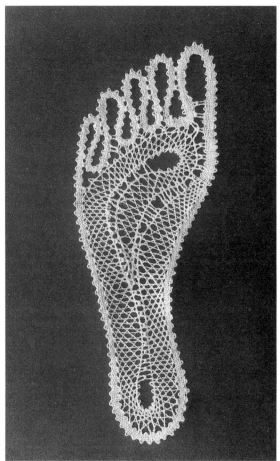

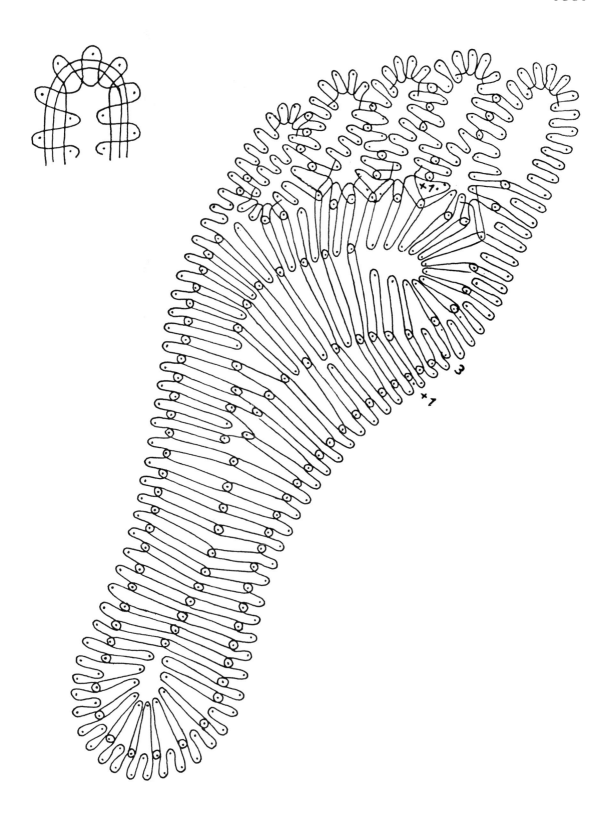

43 Round Leaves

This versatile pattern has rounded leaves and can also be made with rounded corners. It is therefore useful for oval items, mats, collars, etc.

6–7 pairs, linen 35/2

43 Runde Blätter

Nicht nur die Form der Blätter ist rundlich, sondern auch zwei gerundete Ecken gehören dazu – dieses vielseitige Muster eignet besonders für ovale Formen, z.B. Decken, Kragen, usw.

6–7 Paare, Leinen 35/2

43 Les Feuilles rondes

Non seulement la forme des feuilles est ronde, mais il y a aussi deux angles arrondis – ce modèle universel est spécialement indiqué pour les formes ovales, napperons, cols, etc.

6–7 paires, lin 35/2

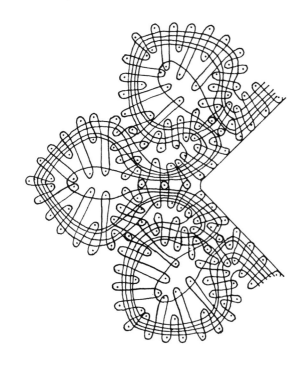

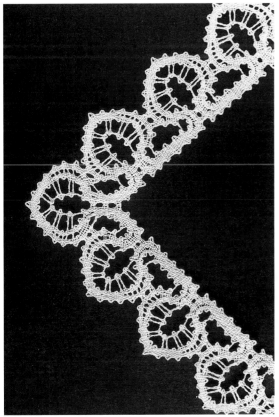

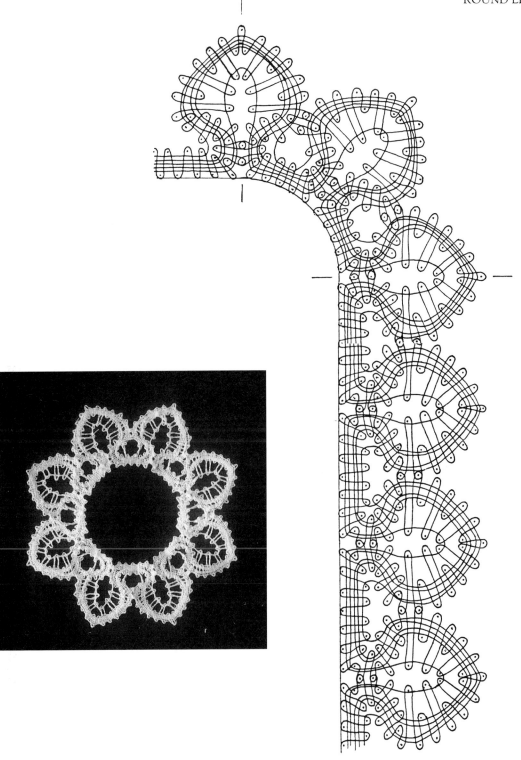

44 Small Bird

A small motif for using up the thread on the bobbins. The bird will sit quite happily on a greetings card, T-shirt, Christmas tree . . . For the version with the 'leaves' on the wings, an auxiliary pair is needed.

7 pairs, linen 60/3

---

44 Kleiner Vogel

Ein kleines Motiv um Fadenreste aufzubrauchen. Der Vogel wird sich wohl fühlen auf einer Glückwunschkarte, auf einem T-shirt, an einem Christbaum . . . Für die Version mit den 'Blättchen' am Flügeln ist ein Hilfspaar nötig.

7 Paare, Leinen 60/3

---

44 Le Petit Oiseau

Un petit motif pour finir le fils des fuseaux. L'oiseau sera à son aise sur une carte de voeux, un t-shirt, un arbre de Noël . . . Pour la version à 'points d'esprit' sur les ailes, une paire auxiliaire est nécessaire.

7 paires, lin 60/3

Small bird and other motifs (16, 36, 37, 41)
Kleiner Vogel und andere Motive (16, 36, 37, 41)
Le petit oiseau et d'autres motifs (16, 36, 37, 41)

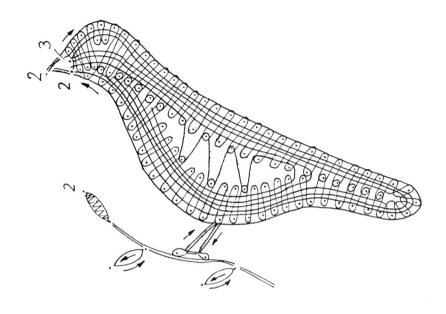

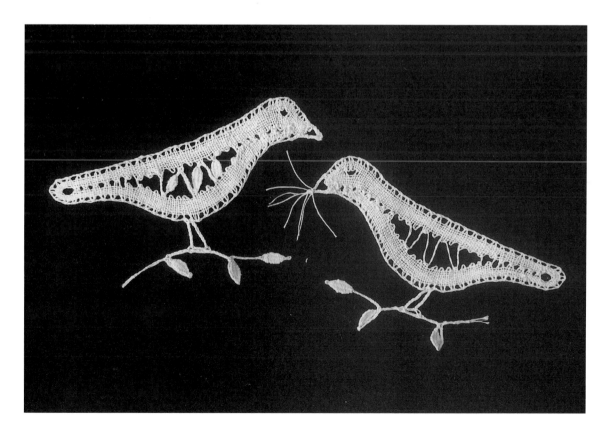

45 Waves

Sometimes ready-made handkerchiefs are not exactly square and it is difficult to adapt the pricking to sides of different lengths. For this pattern the 'waves' are placed around the corner only, and the straight connecting piece is easily shortened. The bobbins beside the mat for a doll's house in photograph 45b are 4.5 cm. ($1\frac{3}{4}''$) long.

45a Handkerchief: 9 pairs, linen 60/3
45b Doll's house mat: 12 pairs, linen 60/2, pricking 85%

45 Wellen

Manchmal sind gekaufte Taschentücher nicht genau quadratisch, und es ist schwierig, den Klöppelbrief an verschieden lange Seiten anzupassen. Bei diesem Muster hat es nur 'Wellen' an den Ecken, der gerade Verbindungsteil lässt sich leicht kürzen. Die Klöppel neben dem Deckchen für die Puppenstube (Fotografie 45b) sind 4,5 cm lang.

45a Taschentuch: 9 Paare, Leinen 60/3
45b Deckchen für die Puppenstube: 12 Paare, Leinen 60/2, Klöppelbrief 85%

45 Les Vagues

Il arrive que les mouchoirs préfabriqués ne soient pas exactement carrés, et il est difficil d'adapter un modèle à des côtés de longueurs inégales. Les 'vagues' de ce modèles se concentrent autour des angles, la partie intermédiaire peut facilement être raccourcie. Les fuseaux à côté du tapis de table pour une chambre de poupée (photographie 45b) mesurent 4,5 cm.

45a Mouchoir: 9 paires, lin 60/3
45b Napperon pour une chambre de poupée: 12 paires, lin 60/2, piquée 85%

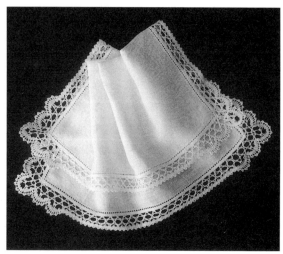

45a

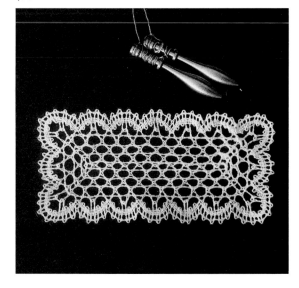

45b

46 Small Triangles

This pattern has not only a variable
length but also a variable depth so that
it will fit any rectangular piece of fabric.
The diagram with plain ground can also
be combined with the previous pattern.

9 or 17 pairs (single or double version),
linen 60/3

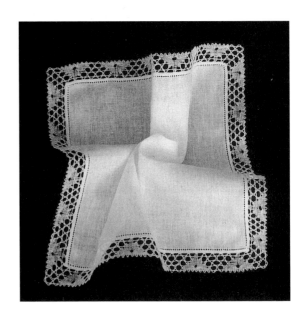

46 Kleine Dreiecke

Dieses Muster hat nicht nur eine variable Länge,
sondern auch eine variable Breite, so dass es an
jedes rechteckige Stück Stoff angepasst werden
kann. Der Klöppelbrief mit dem Grundnetz
kann auch zusammen mit dem vorhergehenden
Muster verwendet werden.

9 oder 17 Paare (einfache oder doppelte
Version), Leinen 60/3

46 Les Petits Triangles

Ce modèle est variable en long et en large, de
manière à pouvoir être adapter à n'importe
quelle pièce de tissu rectangulaire. Le modèle du
fond peut aussi être utilisé avec le modèle
précédant.

9 ou 17 paires (version simple ou double), lin
60/3

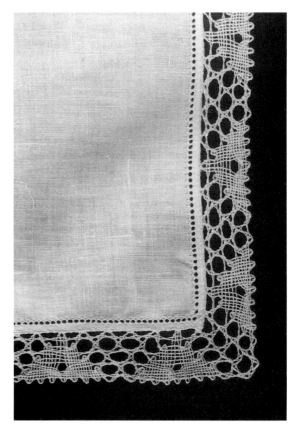

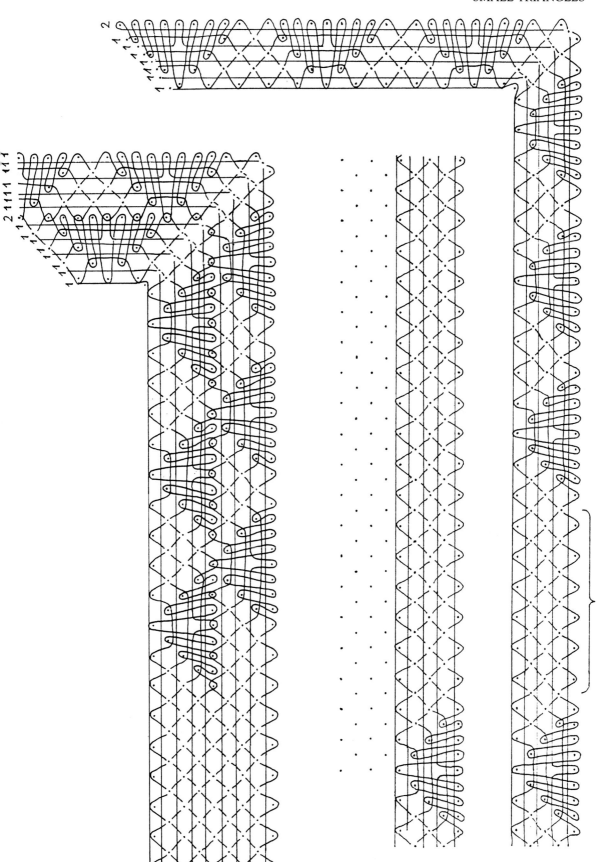

47 Small Dahlia

It may be useful to have a set of round mats of the same size, but with variations in stitches which make the work more interesting. For larger sizes in a matching style see pattern No. 48 (all in lace) and fan pattern No. 9 (lace and fabric).

7 pairs, linen 40/3

47 Kleine Dahlie

Es kann nützlich sein, einen Satz runder Deckchen in der gleichen Grösse zu haben, aber in unterchiedlicher Ausführung, um die Arbeit unterhaltsamer machen. Für grössere Formate im gleichen Stil siehe Muster Nr. 48 (ganz aus Spitze) und Fächermuster Nr. 9 (Spitze und Stoff).

7 Paare, Leinen 40/3

47 Le Petit Dahlia

Il peut être utile d'avoir une serie de napperons ronds de la même grandeur, mais avec des variations dans l'exécution, afin de rendre le travail plus divertissant. Pour les formats plus grands du même style, voir le modèle no 48 (tout en dentelle) ou le modèle de l'éventail no 9 (dentelle et tissu).

7 paires, lin 40/3

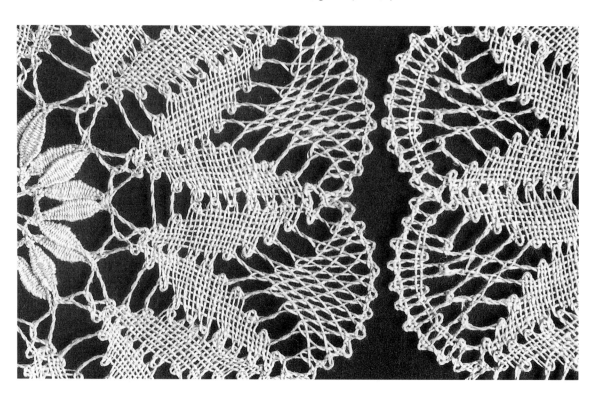

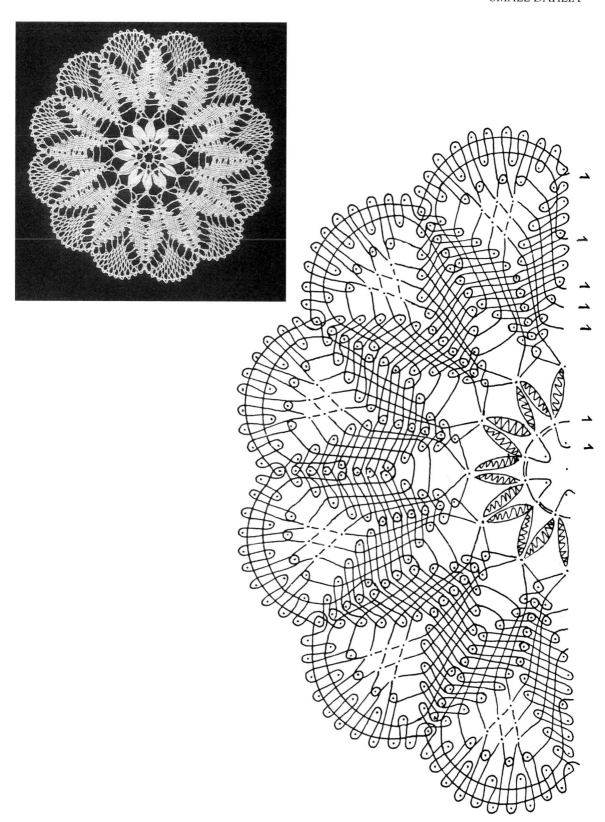

1
1
1 1
1
1 1

48 Large Dahlia

It may be difficult to find round mats of different sizes and of matching styles. The stitches may be varied, as demonstrated in the previous pattern. Ruth Märky has used old lace thread, working on a scaled-down pricking (approx. 64%).

10 pairs, linen 40/3

48 Grosse Dahlie

Es kann schwierig sein, runde Deckchen in verschiedenen Grössen, aber im gleichen Stil zu finden. Die Variationsmöglichkeiten in der Ausführung sind beim vorhergehenden Muster gezeigt. Ruth Märky hat altes Klöppelleinen verwendet auf einem verkleinerten Klöppelbrief (ca. 64%).

10 Paare, Leinen 40/3

48 Le Grand Dahlia

Il peut être difficile de trouver des napperons ronds de différentes grandeurs, mais du même style. Les possibilités de variation dans l'exécution sont présentées par le modèle précédant. Ruth Märky a travaillé avec du fil à dentelle ancien sur un modèle réduit (approx. 64%).

10 paires, lin 40/3

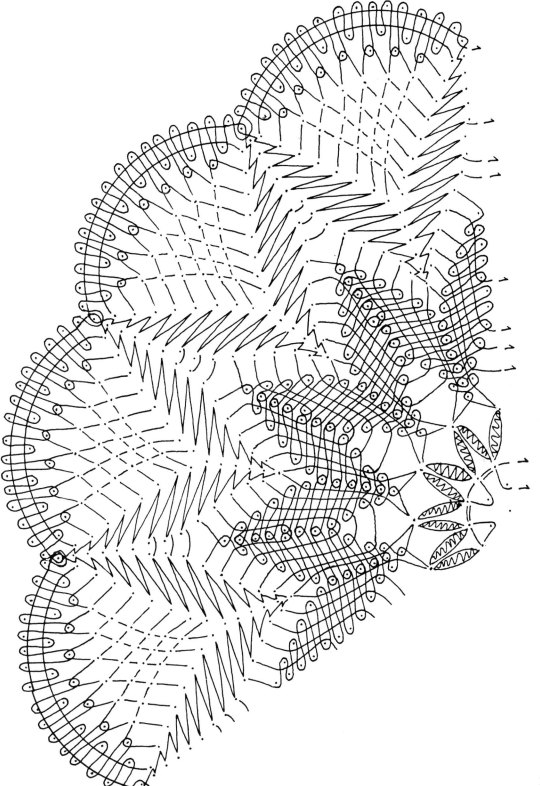

49 Pointed Leaves

The square version (49a) is most suitable
for 3-D motifs. Providing more than
four repeats are worked, these can be
pleated like a fan or gathered in a spiral.
The straight version (49b) can be
combined with pattern No. 30.

49a Square version: 7 pairs, linen 35/2
or 60/3

49b Straight version: 10 pairs, linen
35/2 or 60/3

49a

49 Spitzige Blätter

Das viereckige Muster (49a) ist für
dreidimensionale Motive geeignet, wenn mehr
als vier Rapporte gearbeitet werden, die
fächerförmig gefaltet oder spiralförmige
übereinander gelegt werden. Die gerade Version
(49b) kann mit dem Muster Nr. 30 kombiniert
werden.

49a Viereckige Muster: 7 Paare, Leinen 35/2
oder 60/3

49b Gerade Version: 10 Paare, Leinen 35/2 oder
60/3

49 Les Feuilles pointues

Avec le modèle en carré (49a) il est possible de
confectionner des objets à trois dimensions en
travaillant plus de quatre rapports qui sont pliés
en éventail ou formés en spirale. La version
droite (49b) peut être combinée avec le no 30.

49a Modèle en carré: 7 paires, lin 35/2 ou 60/3
49b Version droite: 10 paires, lin 35/2 ou 60/3

49a

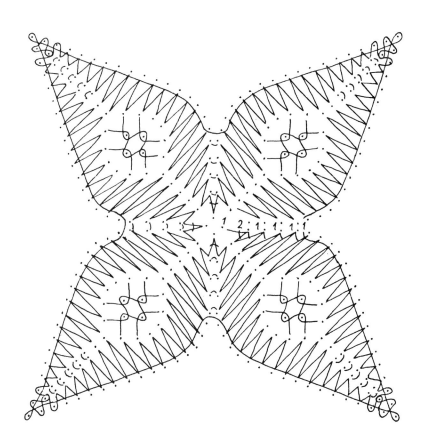

2 2 2 2 1 1

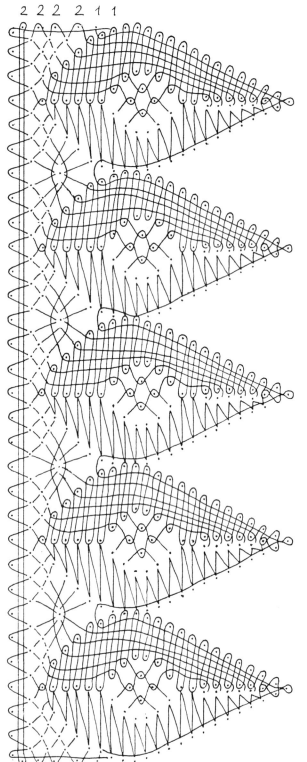

49b

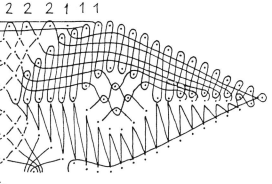

49c Pointed leaves and flowerbuds (pattern 30)
   Spitzige Blätter und Blütenknospen (Muster 30)
   Les feuilles pointues et les boutons de fleur
   (modèle 30)

50 Maze

The central motif is made first, then
pairs are added so that two tapes can be
worked independently, to be joined by
sewings. In some places the tapes can be
worked simultaneously and are joined
simply by workers meeting at the same
pin. The colours must be coordinated
with the background.

12 pairs, linen 35/2

50 Labyrinth

Das Motiv im Zentrum wird zuerst gemacht,
dann werden Paare eingefügt, so dass man mit
zwei unabhängigen Bändchen arbeiten kann, die
zusammengehäkelt werden. An einigen Stellen
sind die zwei Bändchen gleichzeitig geklöppelt
und durch die Laufpaare an der gemeinsamen
Stecknadel verbunden. Die Farben müssen auf
den Hintergrund abgestimmt werden.

12 Paare, Leinen 35/2

50 Le Labyrinthe

Le travail commence par le motif central, puis
des paires sont ajoutées pour obtenir deux lacets
indépendants reliés par des points de raccroc. A
plusieurs endroits les lacets sont faits
simultanément et sont reliés par les 'voyageurs'
qui se rencontrent à la même épingle. Les
couleurs doivent être accordées au ton du fond.

12 paires, lin 35/2

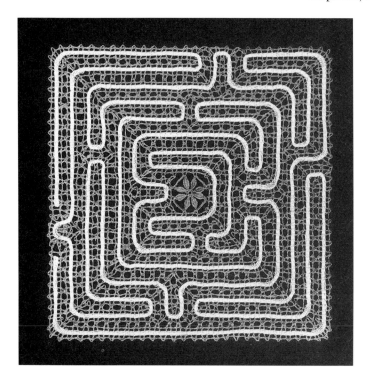

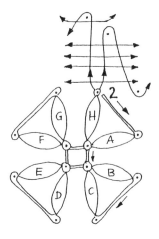

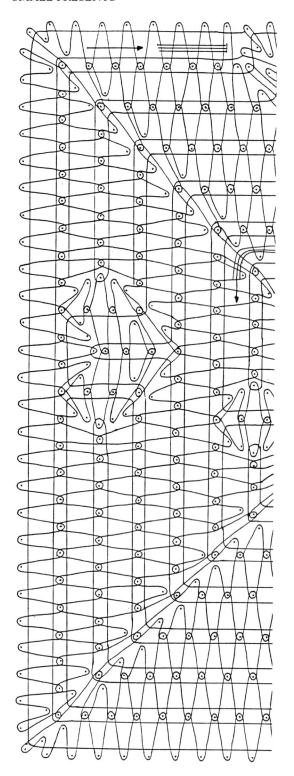

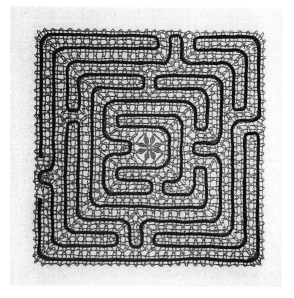

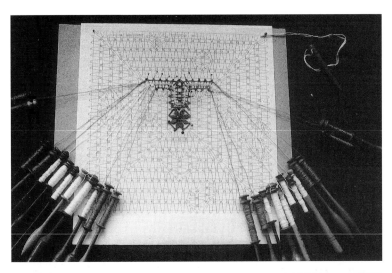

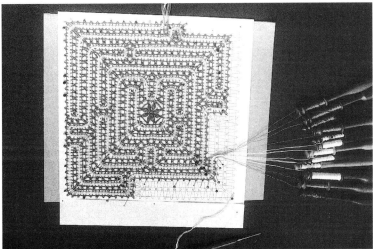

Maze in progress
Labyrinth in Arbeit
Le labyrinthe en exécution

151

BOOK SUPPLIERS

The following are stockists of the complete Batsford/Dryad Press range:

England

AVON
Bridge Bookshop
7 Bridge Street
Bath BA2 4AS

Waterstone & Co.
4–5 Milsom Street
Bath BA1 1DA

BEDFORDSHIRE
Arthur Sells
Lane Cover
49 Pedley Lane
Clifton
Shefford SG17 5QT

BUCKINGHAMSHIRE
J. S. Sear
Lacecraft Supplies
8 Hillview
Sherington MK16 9NJ

CAMBRIDGESHIRE
Dillons the Bookstore
Sidney Street
Cambridge

CHESHIRE
Lynn Turner
Church Meadow Crafts
7 Woodford Road
Winsford

DEVON
Creative Crafts & Needlework
18 High Street
Totnes TQ9 5NP

Honiton Lace Shop
44 High Street
Honiton EX14 8PJ

DORSET
F. Herring & Sons
27 High West Street
Dorchester DT1 1UP

Tim Parker (*mail order*)
124 Corhampton Road
Boscombe East
Bournemouth BH6 5NZ

Christopher Williams
19 Morrison Avenue
Parkstone
Poole BH17 4AD

DURHAM
Lacemaid
6, 10 & 15 Stoneybeck
Bishop Middleham DL17 9BL

GLOUCESTERSHIRE
Southgate Handicrafts
63 Southgate Street
Gloucester GL1 1TX

Waterstone & Company
89–90 The Promenade
Cheltenham GL50 1NB

HAMPSHIRE
Creative Crafts
11 The Square
Winchester SO23 9ES

Doreen Gill
14 Barnfield Road
Petersfield GU31 4DR

Needlestyle
24–26 West Street
Alresford

Ruskins
27 Bell Street
Romsey

ISLE OF WIGHT
Busy Bobbins
Unit 7
Scarrots Lane
Newport PO30 1JD

KENT
The Handicraft Shop
47 Northgate
Canterbury CT1 1BE

Hatchards
The Great Hall
Mount Pleasant Road
Tunbridge Wells

LONDON
W. & G. Foyle Ltd
113–119 Charing Cross Road
WC2H 0EB

Hatchards
187 Piccadilly W1V 9DA

MIDDLESEX
Redburn Crafts
Squires Garden Centre
Halliford Road
Upper Halliford
Shepperton TW17 8RU

NORFOLK
Alby Lace Museum
Cromer Road
Alby
Norwich NR11 7QE

Jane's Pincushions
Taverham Craft Unit 4
Taverham Nursery Centre
Fir Covert Road
Taverham
Norwich NR8 6HT

Waterstone & Company Ltd
30 London Street
Norwich NR2 1LD

NORTH YORKSHIRE
Craft Basics
9 Gillygate
York

Shireburn Lace
Finkle Court
Finkle Hill
Sherburn in Elmet LS25 6EB

The Craft House
23 Bar Street
Scarborough YO13 9QE

SOMERSET
Bridge Bookshop
62 Bridge Street
Taunton TA1 1UD

STAFFORDSHIRE
J. & J. Ford (*mail order & lace days only*)
October Hill
Upper Way
Upper Longdon
Rugeley WS15 1QB

SUSSEX
Waterstone & Company Ltd
120 Terminus Road
Eastbourne

WARWICKSHIRE
Christine & David Springett
21 Hillmorton Road
Rugby CV22 6DF

WEST MIDLANDS
Needlewoman
21 Needles Alley
off New Street
Birmingham B2 5AG

WEST YORKSHIRE
Sebalace
Waterloo Mill
Howden Road
Silsden BD20 0HA

George White Lacemaking
  Supplies
40 Heath Drive
Boston Spa LS23 6PB

Just Lace
Lacemaker Supplies
14 Ashwood Gardens
Gildersome
Leeds LS27 7AS

Jo Firth
58 Kent Crescent
Lowtown, Pudsey
Leeds LS28 9EB

WILTSHIRE
Everyman Bookshop
5 Bridge Street
Salisbury SP1 2ND

Scotland

Embroidery Shop
51 William Street
Edinburgh
Lothian EH3 7LW

Waterstone & Company Ltd
236 Union Street
Aberdeen AB1 1TN

Wales

Bryncraft Bobbins (*mail order*)
B. J. Phillips
Pantglas
Cellan
Lampeter
Dyfed SA48 8JD

Hilkar Lace Suppliers
33 Mysydd Road
Landore
Swansea

EQUIPMENT SUPPLIERS

United Kingdom

BEDFORDSHIRE
A. Sells
49 Pedley Lane
Clifton
Shefford SG17 5QT

BERKSHIRE
Chrisken Bobbins
26 Cedar Drive
Kingsclere RG15 8TD

BUCKINGHAMSHIRE
J. S. Sear
Lacecraft Supplies
8 Hillview
Sherington MK16 9NJ

Winslow Bobbins
70 Magpie Way
Winslow MK18 3PZ

SMP
4 Garners Close
Chalfont St Peter SL9 0HB

CAMBRIDGESHIRE
Josie and Jeff Harrison
Walnut Cottage
Winwick
Huntingdon PE17 5PP

Heffers Graphic Shop (*matt coloured transparent adhesive film*)
26 King Street
Cambridge CB1 1LN

Spangles
Carole Morris
Cashburn Lane
Burwell CB5 0ED

CHESHIRE
Lynn Turner
Church Meadow Crafts
7 Woodford Road
Winsford

DEVON
Honiton Lace Shop
44 High Street
Honiton EX14 8PJ

DORSET
Frank Herring & Sons
27 High West Street
Dorchester DT1 1UP

T. Parker (*mail order, general and bobbins*)
124 Corhampton Road
Boscombe East
Bournemouth BH6 5NZ

ESSEX
Needlework
Ann Bartleet
Bucklers Farm
Coggeshall CO6 1SB

GLOUCESTERSHIRE
T. Brown (*bobbins*)
Temple Lane Cottage
Littledean
Cinderford

Chosen Crafts Centre
46 Winchcombe Street
Cheltenham GL52 2ND

HAMPSHIRE
Busy Bobbins
Unit 7
Scarrots Lane
Newport
IOW
PO30 1JD

Needlestyle
24–26 West Street
Alresford

Newnham Lace Equipment (*lace pillows*)
15 Marlowe Close
Basingstoke RG24 9DD

Richard Viney (*bobbins*)
Unit 7
Port Royal Street
Southsea PO5 3UD

KENT
The Handicraft Shop
47 Northgate
Canterbury CT1 1BE

Denis Hornsby
25 Manwood Avenue
Canterbury CT2 7AH

Frances Iles
73 High Street
Rochester ME1 1LX

LANCASHIRE
Malcolm J. Fielding (*bobbins*)
2 Northern Terrace
Moss Lane
Silverdale LA5 0ST

LINCOLNSHIRE
Ken and Pat Schultz
Whynacres
Shepeau Stow
Whaplode Drove
Spalding PE12 0TU

MERSEYSIDE
Hayes & Finch
Head Office & Factory
Hanson Road
Aintree
Liverpool L9 9BP

155

MIDDLESEX
Redburn Crafts
Squires Garden Centre
Halliford Road
Upper Halliford
Shepperton TW17 8RU

NORFOLK
Alby Lace Museum
Cromer Road
Alby
Norwich NR11 7QE

Jane's Pincushions
Taverham Craft Unit 4
Taverham Nursery Centre
Fir Covert Road
Taverham
Norwich NR8 6HT

George Walker
The Corner Shop
Rickinghall, Diss

NORTH HUMBERSIDE
Teazle Embroideries
35 Boothferry Road
Hull

NORTH YORKSHIRE
The Craft House
23 Bar Street
Scarborough

Shireburn Lace
Finkle Court
Finkle Hill
Sherburn in Elmet LS25 6EB

Stitchery
Finkle Street
Richmond

SOUTH YORKSHIRE
D. H. Shaw
47 Lamor Crescent
Thrushcroft
Rotherham S66 9QD

STAFFORDSHIRE
J. & J. Ford (mail order and lace
    days only)
October Hill
Upper Way
Upper Longdon
Rugeley WS15 1QB

SUFFOLK
A. R. Archer (bobbins)
The Poplars
Shetland
near Stowmarket IP14 3DE

Mary Collins (linen by the metre,
    and made up articles of church
    linen)
Church Furnishings
St Andrews Hall
Humber Doucy Lane
Ipswich IP4 3BP

E. & J. Piper (silk embroidery
    and lace thread)
Silverlea
Flax Lane
Glemsford CO10 7RS

SURREY
Needle and Thread
80 High Street
Horsell
Woking GU21 4SZ

Needlestyle
5 The Woolmead
Farnham GU9 7TX

SUSSEX
Southern Handicrafts
20 Kensington Gardens
Brighton BN1 4AC

WARWICKSHIRE
Christine & David Springett
21 Hillmorton Road
Rugby CV22 5DF

WEST MIDLANDS
Framecraft
83 Hampstead Road
Handsworth Wood
Birmingham B2 1JA

The Needlewoman
21 Needles Alley
off New Street
Birmingham B2 5AE

Stitches
Dovehouse Shopping Parade
Warwick Road
Olton, Solihull

WEST YORKSHIRE
Jo Firth
Lace Marketing & Needlecraft
    Supplies
58 Kent Crescent
Lowtown
Pudsey LS28 9EB

Just Lace
Lacemaker Supplies
14 Ashwood Gardens
Gildersome
Leeds LS27 7AS

Sebalace
Waterloo Mills
Howden Road
Silsden BD20 0HA

George White Lacemaking
    Supplies
40 Heath Drive
Boston Spa LS23 6PB

WILTSHIRE
Doreen Campbell (frames and
    mounts)
Highcliff
Bremilham Road
Malmesbury SN16 0DQ

Scotland

Christine Riley
53 Barclay Street
Stonehaven
Kincardineshire

Peter & Beverley Scarlett
Strupak
Hill Head
Cold Wells, Ellon
Grampian

Wales

Bryncraft Bobbins
B. J. Phillips
Pantglas
Cellan
Lampeter
Dyfed SA48 8JD

Hilkar Lace Suppliers
33 Mysydd Road
Landore
Swansea

Australia

Australian Lace magazine
P.O. Box 609
Manly
NSW 2095

Dentelles Lace Supplies
c/o Betty Franks
39 Lang Terrace
Northgate 4013
Brisbane
Queensland

The Lacemaker
724a Riversdale Road
Camberwell
Victoria 3124

Spindle and Loom
83 Longueville Road
Lane Cove
NSW 2066

Tulis Crafts
201 Avoca Street
Randwick
NSW 2031

Belgium

't Handwerkhuisje
Katelijnestraat 23
8000 Bruges

Kantcentrum
Balstraat 14
8000 Bruges

Manufacture Belge de Dentelle
6 Galerie de la Reine
Galeries Royales St Hubert
1000 Bruxelles

Orchidée
Mariastraat 18
8000 Bruges

Ann Thys
't Apostelientje
Balstraat 11
8000 Bruges

France

Centre d'Enseignement à la
    Dentelle du Puy
2 Rue Duguesclin
43000 Le Puy en Velay

A L'Econome
Anne-Marie Deydier
Ecole de Dentelle aux Fuseaux
10 rue Paul Chenavard
69001 Lyon

Rougier and Plé
13–15 Bd des Filles de Calvaire
75003 Paris

Germany

Barbara Fay
Verlag & Versandbuchhandlung
Am Goosberg 2
D-W 2330 Gammelby

P. P. Hempel
Ortolanweg 34
1000 Berlin

Holland

Blokker's Boektiek
Bronsteeweg 4/4a
2101 AC Heemstede

Theo Brejaart
Dordtselaan 146–148
PO Box 5199
3008 AD Rotterdam

Heikina de Rüyter
Zuiderstraat 1
9693 ER Nieweschans

Magazijn *De Vlijt*
Lijnmarkt 48
Utrecht

Switzerland

Buchhandlung
Dr A. Scheidegger & Co. AG
Obere Bahnhofstr. 10A
CH-8901 Affoltern a.A.

Martin Burkhard
Klöppelzubehör
Jurastrasse 7
CH-5300 Turgi

Fadehax
Inh. Irene Solca
4105 Biel-Benken
Basel

New Zealand

Peter McLeavey
P.O. Box 69.007
Auckland 8

USA

Arbor House
22 Arbor Lane
Roslyn Heights
NY 11577

Baltazor Inc.
3262 Severn Avenue
Metairie
LA 7002

Beggars' Lace
P.O Box 481223
Denver
Colo 80248

Berga Ullman Inc.
P.O. Box 918
North Adams
MA 01247

Happy Hands
3007 S. W. Marshall
Pendleton
Oreg 97180

International Old Lacers Inc
124 West Irvington Place
Denver
CO 80223-1539

The Lacemaker
23732-G Bothell Hwy, SE
Bothell
WA 98021

Lace Place de Belgique
800 S. W. 17th Street
Boca Raton
FL 33432

Lacis
3163 Adeline Street
Berkeley
CA 94703

Robin's Bobbins
RT1 Box 1736
Mineral Bluff
GA 30559-9736

Robin and Russ
Handweavers
533 North Adams Street
McMinnville
Oreg 97128

The Unique And Art Lace
  Cleaners
5926 Delman Boulevard
St Louis
MO 63112

Unicorn Books
Glimakra Looms 'n Yarns Inc.
1304 Scott Street
Petaluma
CA 94954-1181

Van Sciver Bobbin Lace
130 Cascadilla Park
Ithaca
NY 14850

The World in Stitches
82 South Street
Milford
N.H. 03055

SOURCES OF INFORMATION

United Kingdom

The Lace Guild
The Hollies
53 Audnam
Stourbridge
West Midlands DY8 4AE

The Lacemakers' Circle
49 Wardwick
Derby DE1 1HY

The Lace Society
Linwood
Stratford Road
Oversley
Alcester
War BY9 6PG

The British College of Lace
21 Hillmorton Road
Rugby
War CV22 5DF

Ring of Tatters
Miss B. Netherwood
269 Oregon Way
Chaddesden
Derby DE2 6UR

United Kingdom Director of
    International Old Lacers
S. Hurst
4 Dollis Road
London N3 1RG

OIDFA

(International Bobbin and Needle
    Lace Organization)

Hon. President
Kathy Kauffmann
1301 Greenwood
Wilmette
Illinois 60091
USA

Belgium

OIDFA/Belgische Kantorganisatie
Lydia Thiels-Mertens
Jagersberg 1
B-3294 Molenstede-Diest

France

OIDFA
Suzanne Puech
3 Chemin de Parenty
F-69250 Neuville sur Saône

Germany

OIDFA
Uta Ulrich
Papenbergweg 33
D-4930 Detmold

Deutscher Klöppelverband e.V.
Ortolanweg 7
D-1000 Berlin 47

The Netherlands

OIDFA
Puck Smelter-Hoekstra
Corona 68
NL-3204 CM Spijkenisse

LOKK
Boterbloem 56
NL-7322 GX Apeldoorn

Switzerland

FDS
(Fédération de Dentellières
    Suisses)
Evelyne Lütolf
Buhnstrasse 12
CH-8052 Zürich

USA

OIDFA
Kathy Kauffmann
1301 Greenwood
Wilmette
Illinois 60091

International Old Lacers
Gunvor Jorgensen (Pres.)
366 Bradley Avenue
Northvale
NR 076647

Lace & Crafts magazine
3201 East Lakeshore Drive
Tallahassee
FL 32312-2034